BUSH *v.* GORE

ABDO
Publishing Company

BUSH *v.*
GORE

THE FLORIDA RECOUNTS
OF THE 2000 PRESIDENTIAL ELECTION

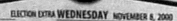

ELECTION EXTRA **WEDNESDAY** NOVEMBER 8, 2000

Orlando
Sentinel

BEST NEWSPAPER IN FLORIDA • FOUNDED 1876

Election 2000 Special

▶ Hillary Clinton wins in N.Y., A13

▶ GOP keeps reins of Senate, A12

▶ State turnout may set record, A11

50 CENTS

orlandosentinel.com

Results

George W. Bush	Al Gore	Ralph Nader
47,101,836 (48%)	47,170,559 (48%)	2,472,939 (3%)

CONTESTED

Florida keeps nation in suspense

by Christine Heppermann

Content Consultant
Richard D. Friedman
Alene and Allan F. Smith Professor of Law
University of Michigan Law School

CREDITS

Published by ABDO Publishing Company, PO Box 398166, Minneapolis, MN 55439. Copyright © 2013 by Abdo Consulting Group, Inc. International copyrights reserved in all countries. No part of this book may be reproduced in any form without written permission from the publisher. The Essential Library™ is a trademark and logo of ABDO Publishing Company.

Printed in the United States of America,
North Mankato, Minnesota
062012
092012

 THIS BOOK CONTAINS AT LEAST 10% RECYCLED MATERIALS.

Editor: Rebecca Rowell
Series Designer: Emily Love
Special thanks to Richard Friedman, Content Consultant for chapters 1–11.

Library of Congress Cataloging-in-Publication Data

Heppermann, Christine.
  Bush v. Gore : the Florida recounts of the 2000 presidential election / by Christine Heppermann ; content consultant Richard D. Friedman.
    p. cm. -- (Landmark Supreme Court cases)
  ISBN 978-1-61783-471-4
  1. Bush, George W. (George Walker), 1946---Trials, litigation, etc.--Juvenile literature. 2. Gore, Albert, 1948---Trials, litigation, etc.--Juvenile literature. 3. United States. Supreme Court--Juvenile literature. 4. Presidents--United States--Election--2000--Juvenile literature. 5. Contested elections--United States--Juvenile literature. 6. Contested elections--Florida--Juvenile literature. 7. Trial and arbitral proceedings I. Friedman, Richard D., 1951- II. Title. III. Title: Bush vs. Gore. IV. Title: Bush versus Gore.
  KF5074.2.H47 2013
  342.73'075--dc23
                            2012001274

Photo Credits

Steve Liss/Time Life Pictures/Getty Images, cover; Peter Cosgrove/AP Images, 3, 17; Red Line Editorial, 9; Ron Edmonds/AP Images, 24; Bruce Weaver/AFP/Getty Images, 27; AP Images, 30, 85; Gary I. Rothstein/AP Images, 32; Wilfredo Lee/AP Images, 35; Adele Starr/AP Images, 36; Dave Martin/AP Images, 44, 65, 82; LM Otero/AP Images, 48; Amy E. Conn/AP Images, 57; Beth A. Keiser/AP Images, 72, 89; Palm Beach Post, Allan Eyestone/AP Images, 74; Alan Diaz/AP Images, 81, 131; Palm Beach Post, Scott Wiseman/AP Images, 97; Charles Archambault/AP Images, 98; Hillery Smith Garrison/AP Images, 111; Anat Givon/AP Images, 118; Harry Cabluck/AP Images, 122; Gerald Herbert/AP Images, 138

Table of Contents

WHAT IS THE US SUPREME COURT?

The US Supreme Court, located in Washington DC, is the highest court in the United States and authorized to exist by the US Constitution. It consists of a chief justice and eight associate justices nominated by the president of the United States and approved by the US Senate. The justices are appointed to serve for life. A term of the court is from the first Monday in October to the first Monday in October the following year.

Each year, the justices are asked to consider more than 7,000 cases. They vote on which petitions they will grant. Four of the nine justices must vote in favor of granting a petition before a case moves forward. Currently, the justices decide between 100 and 150 cases per term.

The justices generally choose cases that address questions of state or federal laws or other constitutional questions they have not previously ruled on. The Supreme Court cannot simply declare a law unconstitutional; it must wait until someone appeals a lower court's ruling on the law.

HOW DOES THE APPEALS PROCESS WORK?

A case usually begins in a local court. For a case involving a federal law, this is usually a federal district court. For a case involving a state or local law, this is a local trial court.

If a defendant is found guilty in a criminal trial and believes the trial court made an error, that person may appeal the case to a higher court. The defendant, now called an appellant, files a brief that explains the error the trial court allegedly made and asks for the decision to be reversed.

An appellate court, or court of appeals, reviews the records of the lower court but does not look at other evidence or call witnesses. If the appeals court finds no errors were made, the appellant may

6

go one step further and petition the US Supreme Court to review the case. A case ruled on in a state's highest court may be appealed to the US Supreme Court.

A Supreme Court decision is based on a majority vote. Occasionally one or more justices will abstain from a case, however, a majority vote by the remaining justices is still needed to overturn a lower-court ruling. What the US Supreme Court decides is final; there is no other court to which a person can appeal. In addition, these rulings set precedent for future rulings. Unless the circumstances are greatly changed, the Supreme Court makes rulings that are consistent with its past decisions. Only an amendment to the US Constitution can overturn a Supreme Court ruling.

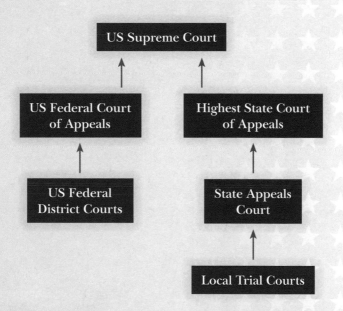

Chapter 1

Not Over Yet

November 7, 2000, was Election Day in the United States. It was a major election: Americans were voting for a new president. Vice President Al Gore was the Democratic candidate. Texas governor George W. Bush was the Republican candidate. The race was heated.

Exit polls forecast narrow margins in many states, but television networks eventually declared Gore and his vice presidential running mate, Senator Joe Lieberman, the victors in much of the Northeast, the Upper Midwest, and California, whereas Bush and running mate Dick Cheney prevailed in Bush's home state of Texas, the South, the mountain states, and the lower Midwest. Soon, it became clear to political analysts from both political parties that the winner

Washington 11
Montana 3
North Dakota 3
Minnesota 10
New Hampshire 4
Vermont 3
Maine 4
Oregon 7
Idaho 4
Wyoming 3
South Dakota 3
Wisconsin 11
Michigan 18
New York 33
Massachusetts 12
Rhode Island 4
Connecticut 8
Nevada 4
Utah 5
Colorado 8
Nebraska 5
Iowa 7
Illinois 22
Indiana 12
Ohio 21
West Virginia 5
Pennsylvania 23
New Jersey 15
Delaware 3
California 54
Kansas 6
Missouri 11
Kentucky 8
Virginia 13
Maryland 10
Washington DC 2*
Arizona 8
New Mexico 5
Oklahoma 8
Arkansas 6
Tennessee 11
North Carolina 14
Alaska 3
Mississippi 7
Alabama 9
Georgia 13
South Carolina 8
Texas 32
Louisiana 9
Florida 25
Hawaii 4

Key
■ Gore
■ Bush

* The District of Columbia has three votes. One elector chose not to vote.

This map shows which presidential candidate won each state on November 7, 2000, and how many electoral votes were allotted to each state.

of the 2000 presidential election would be the man who won the state that had seemed to swing one way and then the other all night long: Florida. The Sunshine State became the focus of the election because each candidate needed Florida's 25 electoral votes to capture the presidency.

9

EXIT POLLS

An exit poll is a survey given to voters as they leave polling places that asks them how they voted in the various races on the ballot. Usually conducted by private companies hired by news organizations, exit polls help the media forecast which candidates will win before returns are officially tallied, a process that can take hours or even days. Exit polls also collect demographic data to discover which candidates certain groups—women, for instance, or African Americans—tend to support. All votes in the United States are cast anonymously, and no voter is required to participate in an exit poll.

In the United States, citizens cast their votes for the president, but electors ultimately choose the winning candidate in a process established by the US Constitution. These electors make up the Electoral College and cast the electoral votes that are allotted to each state. In general, the candidate who wins the most popular votes—the most votes of the people—in each state wins all of that state's electoral votes. The number of electors allocated to each state equals its number of US senators—always two—and US representatives, which is based on population. The higher a state's population, the more US representatives it has and the more electors it has in the Electoral College. So, for instance, Gore's win in California, the most populous state, netted him 54 electoral votes, but his win in Oregon earned him only 7.[1]

THE ELECTORAL COLLEGE

At the Constitutional Convention in Philadelphia, Pennsylvania, in 1787, delegates debated over what process to establish for selecting a president. Many delegates wanted the newly formed Congress—the Senate and the House of Representatives—to take on this responsibility. These delegates feared that ordinary voters, who were mainly white males, were not informed enough to be trusted with such an important decision. Information traveled slowly in those days. There was no radio, no television, no Internet, and only a handful of newspapers. Some delegates worried the general population could not learn enough about presidential candidates to figure out who would make an effective leader. But some delegates objected to giving Congress this much power. They believed any president Congress chose would be under its sway. The framers of the Constitution worked out a compromise, set forth in Article II, Section 1. Each state would be assigned electors based on its number of representatives in Congress: two senators per state and, depending on a state's population, one or more representatives. The legislature of each state would determine how the electors were chosen. Not all electors are required to vote the same as the popular vote.

A presidential candidate needs 270 electoral votes to emerge victorious. With all states but Florida decided, Gore had 266 electoral votes and Bush had 246.[2] Whichever of the two candidates won the popular vote in Florida would become the forty-third president of the United States.

CANDIDATES' REASONS FOR HOPE AND DOUBT IN FLORIDA

Gore and Bush had reasons for optimism and pessimism in their battle to win Florida. In Bush's favor, Republican presidential candidates had won the state in all but three elections during the past 40 years. Republicans controlled the state legislature, and Bush's younger brother Jeb Bush was the governor and rallied support from the governor's office. Northern Florida, more rural and conservative than the flashy, glittering cities of the south, seemed within Bush's grasp. And the large Cuban immigrant population still harbored animosity against President Bill Clinton and the Democrats for the extradition of Elián González, a young Cuban refugee ordered back to Cuba by the courts earlier in the year. Gore, on the other hand, could hope for votes from the state's ever-growing black, Hispanic, and Jewish voters, as well as from the numerous retirees who had relocated from New York City and other highly Democratic urban areas.

No Quick Results

Americans eagerly watching the election results on their televisions could not help but be confused when newscasters could not seem to figure out what exactly was going on with the Florida polls. At approximately 8:00 p.m. eastern standard time, the networks projected from exit-poll interviews that Gore had taken Florida. However, not all votes were in. Polls in the eastern part of the state had closed, but Florida's Panhandle stretches into the central time zone, so residents there had another hour to cast their ballots. At 2:16 a.m. eastern standard time, exhausted, bleary-eyed news anchors announced they had made a mistake: Bush was the winner in Florida and had won the presidency.

From his family's suite on the ninth floor of the Loews Vanderbilt Hotel in downtown Nashville, Tennessee, Gore called Bush at the governor's mansion in Austin, Texas, to concede the election and offer his congratulations. The call lasted less than two minutes.

A dejected crowd of Gore supporters lingered in Nashville's War Memorial Plaza while the vice president's motorcade wended toward them through the dark, drizzly streets. All night, they had waited for their candidate to walk on stage and give a speech. But they had hoped for and expected a victory celebration, not a concession. Still, they waited to cheer for and sympathize with the man who had come so close to heading the nation.

They waited and waited, wondering where Gore was. He was actually quite close by, in a basement office at the War Memorial, preparing to make another telephone call. Before he could climb the steps to the stage, one of his aides, David Morehouse, intercepted Gore to tell him the margin of votes in Florida was now confirmed to be fewer than 2,000. That figure meant the difference in votes cast for each candidate was less than one-half of 1 percent of the total votes cast for president. Under Florida election code, this development mandated a machine recount. All ballots were required to be put through the tabulation machines again.

No Concession

An hour after Gore called Bush to concede, he called the Texas governor again. Witnesses from both parties have said the candidates' conversation went something like this:

Gore: "Circumstances have changed dramatically since I first called you. The state of Florida is too close to call."

Bush: "Are you saying what I think you're saying? Let me make sure that I understand. You're calling back to retract the concession?"

Gore: "You don't have to be snippy about it."[3]

ELECTION DAY

A president is elected every four years. In the United States, general elections are held the Tuesday after the first Monday in November. This schedule means the earliest an election can be held is November 2 and the latest is November 8. Congress chose this day in 1845. Initially, there was not a specific day for national elections. Rather, there was a broader time frame. States simply had to hold their elections for president sometime in the 34 days before the Electoral College met, which was the first Wednesday in December. November was selected because, at the time, most Americans lived on farms and harvesting would have been completed but snow would not have yet closed roads. Tuesday was selected because it was argued to be the first day of the week voters could get to the polls, which were in towns: people would have been in church on Sunday, and voters living in very rural areas would have spent Monday traveling.

Bush explained that his younger brother Jeb, the governor of Florida, assured him he had won the state. Gore fired back, "Let me explain something. Your little brother is not the ultimate authority on this."[4]

Election Day had come to an end, but the race was not over yet. Rather, a legal battle was beginning that would decide the presidency. For the next 36 days, Florida would hold the attention of the nation and the world while the winner of the state's popular vote remained in dispute. This fight for the nation's highest office would ultimately be decided in the nation's highest court in a landmark case that would make history. ～

> **We don't just have egg on our face, we have an omelette on our suits."[5]**
> —*TOM BROKAW, ANCHOR FOR THE NBC EVENING NEWS, ABOUT THE MEDIA MISCALLING THE ELECTION*

Oh, so close

Presidential race knotted in wee hours

METRO WEDNESDAY NOVEMBER 8, 2000

Orlando Sentinel

Election 2000 Special
▸ Hillary Clinton wins in N.Y., A13
▸ GOP keeps reins of Senate, A12
▸ State turnout may set record, A11

50 cents

THE BEST NEWSPAPER IN FLORIDA · FOUNDED 1876

Results	George W. Bush 43,665,308 (49%)	Al Gore 43,062,885 (48%)	Ralph Nader 2,269,088 (3%)

IT'S BUSH

Florida puts Republican over top in nail-biter

WEDNESDAY NOVEMBER 8, 2000

Orlando Sentinel

Election 2000 Special
▸ Hillary Clinton wins in N.Y., A13
▸ GOP keeps reins of Senate, A12
▸ State turnout may set record, A11

50 cents

THE BEST NEWSPAPER IN FLORIDA · FOUNDED 1876

Results	George W. Bush 45,938,645 (48%)	Al Gore 45,843,630 (48%)	Ralph Nader 2,472,939 (3%)

IS IT BUSH ?

Florida vote leaves Republican's win in doubt

ELECTION EXTRA WEDNESDAY NOVEMBER 8, 2000

Orlando Sentinel

Election 2000 Special
▸ Hillary Clinton wins in N.Y., A13
▸ GOP keeps reins of Senate, A12
▸ State turnout may set record, A11

50 CENTS

THE BEST NEWSPAPER IN FLORIDA · FOUNDED 1876

Results	George W. Bush 47,101,836 (48%)	Al Gore 47,170,559 (48%)	Ralph Nader 2,472,939 (3%)

CONTESTED

Florida keeps nation in suspense

On November 8, 2000, the *Orlando Sentinel* printed four different editions covering the presidential election results.

Chapter 2

A Tight Race

The 2000 presidential election had come down to a virtual tie between two very different men with similar backgrounds. Both had attended Ivy League universities, and they were 50-something-year-old white men from prominent political families.

Although Gore's family hailed from Tennessee, the future vice president was born and raised in Washington DC. There, his father represented Tennessee as a congressman and then a US senator. Gore followed this career path. He won a seat in the US House of Representatives in 1976, served four terms, and then moved on to the US Senate, serving from 1985 to 1993.

Bush's father had also served as a member of Congress. He was a representative from Texas for two terms. He was not successful in his attempt to become a senator, but George H. W. Bush held other important government positions, including ambassador to the United Nations and director of the Central Intelligence Agency. Then, he went on to serve in even higher public offices. George H. W. Bush served as vice president during Ronald Reagan's two terms in office: 1981–1989. In 1988, the elder Bush was elected the forty-first president of the United States. He served from 1989 to 1993. In addition, George's younger brother Jeb Bush rose through the ranks of Florida politics and was elected governor of the state in 1998.

Gore's Relationship with Clinton

Many political analysts believed Gore should have had a smooth road to the presidency. He served two terms as vice president under Bill Clinton (1993–2001), who was popular and considered charismatic by many. And the years of Clinton's presidency were during a period of relative economic prosperity. When Clinton first took office in January 1993, the national debt stood at a record level. By the end of Clinton's second term, that debt had turned into a surplus. Unemployment rates were down and tax revenues were up. Exit polls on Election Day in 2000 revealed that, for the most part, Americans felt confident about the state of the economy. By all accounts, Gore should have ridden this wave of public satisfaction to a comfortable victory.

Yet Gore had actually worked to distance himself from Clinton in voters' minds. Despite the sound economy, personal scandal marred the Clinton presidency, and Gore did not want to tarnish himself by association. Clinton and his wife had been accused of improper real estate dealings in a controversy dubbed "Whitewater," the name of the Arkansas development project in which the Clintons and some friends had invested. In addition, the president had engaged in an extramarital relationship with Monica Lewinsky, a woman who had interned at the White House. On December 19, 1998, the House of Representatives voted to **impeach** Clinton after a **grand jury** found him guilty

---

grand jury—A group of people selected to examine the charges against a suspect and determine if that suspect should be charged with a crime for which the suspect will be later tried.

impeach—To accuse someone in public office of wrongdoing; it is the first step in trying to remove that person from office.

of perjury, or lying under oath, and obstructing the investigation of his relationship with Lewinsky.

Not wanting voters to think he approved of Clinton's behavior, Gore allowed the president to campaign for him in only two states: Arkansas and West Virginia. Later, pundits would call this strategy a mistake. They said Americans were more forgiving than Gore assumed and campaigning by the likable Clinton in Florida and other key states might have gained Gore the votes he needed to win.

Image Problems

Gore and Bush each suffered from unique image problems during the campaign. Gore did not have the natural social ease of Bush or Clinton. In speeches, Gore often came across as stiff and humorless. He also had a reputation for being a know-it-all intellectual— a commonly repeated misquote from a 1999 CNN interview was that he claimed to have invented the Internet. Gore's attempts to loosen up, critics generally agreed, made him look silly.

Bush, on the other hand, was popularly described as the candidate the average American would most want to have a beer with. People warmed to his laid-back personality. However, some people questioned his intellect. He had a tendency to muddle words—"misunderestimated" is one of his more famous coinages—mispronounce world leaders' names, and spout nonsensical sentences.[1] When questioned about domestic or foreign policy issues, he sometimes seemed to struggle to grasp the details.

The Presidential Debates

Observers agreed the three presidential debates, all held in October 2000, improved public perception of Bush and made Gore look like an actor unable to decide which character he was supposed to be playing. Gore rolled his eyes. He also got very close to Bush, invading

BUSHISMS

Bush's creative way with language has led to many Bushisms—words and comments that are uniquely his own. The press recorded several during his presidential campaign. On January 3, 2000, Bush claimed, "One of the great things about books is sometimes there are some fantastic pictures."[2] On August 30, he stated, "Well, I think if you say you're going to do something and don't do it, that's trustworthiness."[3] And on September 6, Bush said, "We'll let our friends be the peacekeepers and the great country called America will be the pacemakers."[4]

his personal space. Both of these actions were rude. Neither of them was presidential.

Some thought Gore would say just about anything to win the election. As a result of the debates, some Americans trusted him less than Bush. While Gore appeared to flip-flop personalities, Bush surprised viewers by avoiding major blunders and displaying a better understanding of the issues than he had shown in previous appearances. Still, Bush was not the perfect candidate in the days before the election.

Last-Minute Campaigning

Some political analysts have claimed Bush grew complacent with his apparent lead in the polls. As Gore

Debates play an important role in presidential races by giving viewers a sense of the candidates' personalities and their positions on issues.

tirelessly toured the country until Election Day, visiting as many swing states as he could, Bush's schedule of appearances was less rigorous. He took off a Sunday within weeks of the election.

Bush's choices for last-minute campaigning may have affected the election results as well. He breezed in and out of California and New Jersey, Democratic strongholds he had little chance of winning, instead of stopping in Florida. Had he visited the state, the margin of votes there may have been larger. Maybe his lead on the day after the election would not have stood where it did: a mere 1,784 votes.[5] But the candidates made the decisions they did, and so did the voters. The result was one of the closest presidential races in US history, and it all came down to Florida. ∿

THE TWELFTH AMENDMENT

The United States has weathered other extremely close, controversial presidential elections. In 1800, Thomas Jefferson and Aaron Burr, both Republicans, tied for the most votes in the Electoral College. Under the original system, each elector cast votes for two people. Candidates did not run for vice president. Rather, the candidate who received the most votes, so long as he was named by a majority, became president. The man who got the second most became vice president. The tiebreaking vote was given to the House of Representatives, with each state's delegation casting one vote. At that time, the House was controlled by the opposing party: the Federalists. After 36 rounds of voting, some Federalists relented and gave Jefferson the majority needed to win. Burr became vice president.

This less-than-perfect election led to the Twelfth Amendment. Ratified in 1804, it gave each elector in the Electoral College two distinct votes—one for president and one for vice president. The ratification of this amendment meant the runner-up in the presidential election would no longer be named vice president. If no candidate wins a majority of votes, the House elects the president. The Senate elects the vice president.

Chapter 3

Ballot Issues

On November 8, 2000, the day after the presidential election, concerns about the results were spreading across the nation. But there had been local concerns in Florida on Election Day. On November 7, two voters arrived at the office of Theresa LePore in West Palm Beach to complain about the ballot. LePore was election supervisor for Florida's Palm Beach County. "We thought it was an isolated incident, because they were a couple of very elderly gentlemen," LePore recalled in a 2001 interview.[1] But this was not the case.

The Butterfly Ballot

As election supervisor, LePore selected the ballot design for her constituency. The ballot's layout

BALLOT, GENERAL ELECTION
BEACH COUNTY, FLORIDA
NOVEMBER 7, 2000

OFFICIAL BALLOT, GENERAL ELE*
PALM BEACH COUNTY, FLOR*
NOVEMBER 7, 2000

(REPUBLICAN)
GEORGE W. BUSH - PRESIDENT 3▶
DICK CHENEY - VICE PRESIDENT

(DEMOCRATIC)
AL GORE - PRESIDENT 5▶
JOE LIEBERMAN - VICE PRESIDENT

(LIBERTARIAN)
HARRY BROWNE - PRESIDENT 7▶
ART OLIVIER - VICE PRESIDENT

(GREEN)
RALPH NADER - PRESIDENT 9▶
WINONA LaDUKE - VICE PRESIDENT

(SOCIALIST WORKERS)
JAMES HARRIS - PRESIDENT 11▶
MARGARET TROWE - VICE PRESIDENT

(NATURAL LAW)
JOHN HAGELIN - PRESIDENT 13▶
NAT GOLDHABER - VICE PRESIDENT

◀4 **(REFORM)**
PAT BUCHANAN - PRESIDENT
EZOLA FOSTER - VICE PRESIDENT

◀6 **(SOCIALIST)**
DAVID McREYNOLDS - PRESIDENT
MARY CAL HOLLIS - VICE PRESIDENT

◀8 **(CONSTITUTION)**
HOWARD PHILLIPS - PRESIDENT
J. CURTIS FRAZIER - VICE PRESIDENT

◀10 **(WORKERS WORLD)**
MONICA MOOREHEAD - PRESIDENT
GLORIA La RIVA - VICE PRESIDENT

WRITE-IN CANDIDATE
To vote for a write-in candidate, follow the
directions on the long stub of your ballot card.

Palm Beach County's 2000 presidential ballot—the butterfly
ballot—became a point of much debate and anger.

involved two adjacent pages that opened like wings to
reveal two columns of candidate names. Between the
columns was a line of holes labeled with numbered
arrows that indicated which hole to punch for which
candidate. The ballot resembled a butterfly, so that was
what the press began calling it—the butterfly ballot. No
other Florida county used this ballot format in 2000.

27

The butterfly ballot left a number of Palm Beach voters confused, anxious, and, in the end, angry. They walked out of their polling places wondering if they had voted for the candidate they meant to vote for or if they had mistakenly punched the wrong hole. Soon, telephone lines at LePore's office were jammed with calls from people worried they had made a mistake. Many demanded they be allowed to revote.

Ironically, LePore had chosen the butterfly ballot design because she thought it would be easy to read. Palm Beach County has a large number of elderly residents. Cramming the names of all ten presidential candidates and their running mates—Bush/Cheney, Gore/Lieberman, and eight minor-party tickets—onto

FIGHTING THE BUTTERFLY BALLOT

On November 8, 2000, three Palm Beach County residents filed a lawsuit. In the suit, the residents claimed the butterfly ballot was illegal. They proposed a solution: reprint the ballots in a new format and hold another election using the new ballots. A circuit court judge denied their request, noting he had no authority to call a new election. The ballot remained a sore spot for many who felt that, without it, Gore would have prevailed on Election Day. The case, *Fladell v. LaBarga* (2000), was one of many filed regarding ballots.

THE RESIDENTS OF PALM BEACH COUNTY

Palm Beach County is one of Florida's largest counties. West Palm Beach, the county seat, is the largest city in the county. Other cities in Palm Beach County include Boca Raton, Boynton Beach, Delray Beach, Jupiter, and Wellington. At the time of the 2000 census, the county had 1,131,184 residents.[3] Palm Beach County had a large senior population, with 23.2 percent of the residents aged 65 years old or older.[4] Florida had the highest population of senior citizens among all US states: 17.6 percent.[5]

one page required very small type. LePore thought print so small would be difficult for older voters to see clearly. Dividing the names into two columns allowed for larger, more readable type. A few weeks before the election, as was customary, LePore's office mailed sample ballots to local party officials and other groups, including all of the county's 655,000 registered voters.[2] She received no objections. All seemed ready to go.

But almost as soon as the polls opened in Palm Beach County, voters started making panicked calls to LePore's office. Most were elderly Democrats who feared they had accidentally voted for Reform Party candidate Patrick Buchanan instead of Gore. The ballot listed Gore and Lieberman in the first column, directly underneath Bush and Cheney, with Buchanan and running mate

GENERAL ELECTION
ORANGE COUNTY FLORIDA
NOVEMBER 7, 2000
TO VOTE, COMPLETE THE ARROW: ← ■
POINTING TO YOUR CHOICE: ← ■

ELECCION GENERAL
CONDADO DE ORANGE, FLORIDA
EL 7 DE NOVIEMBRE DE 2000
PARA VOTAR, COMPLETE LA FLECHA: ← ■
QUE APUNTA A SU SELECCION: ← ■

If you tear, deface or wrongly mark this ballot, return it and get another. Mark with Pencil or Pen (No Red Ink).
Si usted rompe, estropea o incorrectamente marca esta papeleta, devuelva y pida otra. Marque con Lápiz o Tinto (No Tinta Roja).

ELECTORS FOR PRESIDENT & VICE-PRESIDENT
ELECTORES PARA PRESIDENTE & VICE PRESIDENTE
(A vote for the candidate will actually be a vote for their electors)
(Vote for Group)
(Un voto para el candidato sera un voto para su voto en el groupo electo)
(Vote por el groupo)

REPUBLICAN
George W. BUSH (Pres) ← ■
Dick CHENEY (V.-Pres)

DEMOCRAT
Al GORE (Pres) ← ■
Joe LIEBERMAN (V.-Pres)

LIBERTARIAN
Harry BROWNE (Pres) ← ■
Art OLIVIER (V. Pres)

GREEN PARTY
Ralph NADER (Pres) ← ■
Winona LADUKE (V. Pres)

SOCIALIST WORKERS PARTY
James HARRIS (Pres) ← ■
Margaret TROWE (V. Pres)

NATURAL LAW PARTY
John HAGELIN (Pres) ← ■
Nat GOLDHABER (V. Pres)

REFORM PARTY
Pat BUCHANAN (Pres) ← ■
Ezola FOSTER (V. Pres)

SOCIALIST PARTY
David MCREYNOLDS (Pres) ← ■
Mary Cal HOLLIS (V. Pres)

CONSTITUTION PARTY OF FLA
Howard PHILLIPS (Pres) ← ■
J. Curtis FRAZIER (V. Pres)

WORKERS WORLD PARTY
Monica MOOREHEAD (Pres) ← ■
Gloria LA RIVA (V. Pres)

WRITE-IN
_____ (Pres) ← ■
_____ (V. Pres)

All Registered Voters vote on the above Race

CONGRESSIONAL
CONGRESIONAL
U.S. SENATOR
SENADOR FEDERAL
(Vote for One) (Vote por Uno)

Bill MCCOLLUM (REP) ← ■
Bill NELSON (DEM) ← ■
SIMONETTA (LAW) ← ■
DECKARD (REF) ← ■
_____ (LOG) ← ■
MARTIN _____
MCCORMICK (NPA) ← ■

U.S. REPRESENTATIVE
REPRESENTANTE, U.S.
DISTRICT 3   DISTRITO 3
(Vote for One) (Vote por Uno)

Jennifer S. CARROLL (REP) ← ■
Corrine BROWN (DEM) ← ■
_____ (WRI) ← ■

All Registered Voters in U.S. Representative District 3 vote on the above Race

U.S. REPRESENTATIVE
REPRESENTANTE, U.S.
DISTRICT 7   DISTRITO 7
(Vote for One) (Vote por Uno)

John L. MICA (REP) ← ■
Dan VAUGHEN (DEM) ← ■
_____ (WRI) ← ■

All Registered Voters in U.S. Representative District 7 vote on the above Race

U.S. REPRESENTATIVE
REPRESENTANTE, U.S.
DISTRICT 8   DISTRITO 8
(Vote for One) (Vote por Uno)

Ric KELLER (REP) ← ■
Linda W. CHAPIN (DEM) ← ■
_____ (WRI) ← ■

All Registered Voters in U.S. Representative District 8 vote on the above Race

STATE   ESTADO
TREASURER   TESORERO
(Vote for One) (Vote por Uno)

Tom GALLAGHER (REP) ← ■
John COSGROVE (DEM) ← ■

All Registered Voters vote on the above Race

COMMISSIONER OF EDUCATION
COMISIONADO DE EDUCACION
(Vote for One) (Vote por Uno)

Charlie CRIST (REP) ← ■
George H. SHELDON (DEM) ← ■
Vassilia GAZETAS (NPA) ← ■

All Registered Voters vote on the above Race

PUBLIC DEFENDER
DEFENSOR DE PUBLICO
(Vote for One) (Vote por Uno)

Letty MARQUES (REP) ← ■
Bob WESLEY (DEM) ← ■

All Registered Voters vote on the above Race

LEGISLATIVE
LEGISLATIVO
STATE SENATOR
SENADOR DEL ESTADO
DISTRICT 9   DISTRITO 9
(Vote for One) (Vote por Uno)

Lee CONSTANTINE (REP)
Ron ELLMAN (DEM)

All Registered Voters in State Senate District 9 vote on the above Race

STATE REPRESENTATIVE
REPRESENTANTE ESTATAL
DISTRICT 32   DISTRITO 32
(Vote for One) (Vote por Uno)

Bob ALLEN (REP) ←
Joe Lee SMITH (DEM) ←

All Registered Voters in State Representative District 32 vote on the above Race

STATE REPRESENTATIVE
REPRESENTANTE ESTATAL
DISTRICT 33   DISTRITO 33
(Vote for One) (Vote por Uno)

Tom FEENEY (REP) ←
Glenda CONLEY (DEM) ←

All Registered Voters in State Representative District 33 vote on the above Race

STATE REPRESENTATIVE
REPRESENTANTE ESTATAL
DISTRICT 34   DISTRITO 34
(Vote for One) (Vote por Uno)

David J. MEALOR (REP) ←
'Dr. Andy' MICHAUD (DEM) ←

All Registered Voters in State Representative District 34 vote on the above Race

STATE REPRESENTATIVE
REPRESENTANTE ESTATAL
DISTRICT 35   DISTRITO 35
(Vote for One) (Vote por Uno)

Jim KALLINGER (REP) ←
James 'Jimmy' AUFFANT (DEM) ←

All Registered Voters in State Representative District 35 vote on the above Race

STATE REPRESENTATIVE
REPRESENTANTE ESTATAL
DISTRICT 36   DISTRITO 36
(Vote for One) (Vote por Uno)

Allen TROVILLION (REP) ←
Alana BRENNER (DEM) ←
_____ (WRI) ←

Ballot design varied across Florida. This is a sample ballot from Orlando, where manual recounts were not requested.

Ezola Foster topping the column on the facing page. Punching the second hole in the center line registered a vote for Buchanan/Foster. Punching the third hole registered a vote for Gore/Lieberman. In response to the complaints, LePore's office issued a memo late Tuesday morning to all 531 of the county's voting precincts.[6] The memo said,

> *Please remind all voters . . . they are to vote for only one (1) presidential candidate and that they are to punch the hole next to the arrow next to the number next to the candidate they wish to vote for. Thank you!"*[7]

Apparently, not everyone got the message. And some voters who had already cast their ballots were worried—or even certain—they had done it incorrectly.

When all the results were in, largely Democratic Palm Beach County ended up giving ultraconservative candidate Buchanan 3,407 votes.[8] That was more votes than he received in any Florida county—more than 2,000 more than he received in his second-best showing, Pinellas County, the home of his campaign headquarters.[9] Outraged Democrats pointed fingers at LePore's ballot, and, given the numbers, it was hard to challenge them. Buchanan himself acknowledged some

Floridians protested the butterfly ballot outside the Palm Beach County elections office in West Palm Beach on November 9, 2000.

percentage of his Palm Beach votes had likely been meant for Gore.

The possibility of mistakenly supporting Buchanan particularly irritated the county's sizable Jewish population, voters who had welcomed the opportunity to vote for Lieberman, the first Jew nominated by a major party for vice president. They also believed Buchanan was prejudiced against Jewish people, and they could hardly bear the thought of marking their ballots for someone with his alleged beliefs.

Another indication of voter confusion was Palm Beach County's larger-than-average number of "overvotes," ballots on which the voter had selected two or more candidates for president, thus rendering the ballots invalid. Many overvotes showed holes punched for both Gore and Buchanan. Perhaps bewildered Democratic voters punched the hole for Buchanan and then, realizing their error, punched the hole for Gore. Bush did not escape this problem. Palm Beach voters also punched holes for both Bush and Buchanan on the same ballot.

Hanging Chad

While LePore struggled with the issue of the butterfly ballot, another issue came to light. The hanging chad was the subject of much debate. A chad is a tiny scrap of paper that is a by-product of punch-card voting systems. It is usually discarded.

The problem was that chads did not always detach. Voting equipment in Florida—and in much of the

United States—remained relatively primitive in 2000. Despite advances in computer technology, 25 of Florida's 67 counties, including Palm Beach, still relied on punch-card machines originally designed at the end of the nineteenth century.[10] Other counties used an optical-scan voting system in which voters darkened ovals on their ballots with a pen or pencil, the way students often do on standardized tests, and then put them through tabulation scanners. The Votomatic and other punch-card machines required voters to push a metal stylus through paper to make their marks.

Punch-card voting systems have multiple steps to operate. First, a voter inserts a punch card into a hollow holder with a pin on each side to keep the card in place.

TYPES OF CHAD

Chads often detached fully from ballots. Those that did not acquired many different adjectives in the press in 2000. A dimpled or pregnant chad occurs when the stylus indents the chad but does not dislodge it. Instead, there is an impression on one side of the ballot and a bump on the other. A pinprick occurs when light can be seen through a small hole in the chad, which remains on the ballot, having not been fully detached by the stylus. A hanging or detached chad occurs when a stylus detaches the chad but does not push it cleanly off the ballot, leaving it hanging.

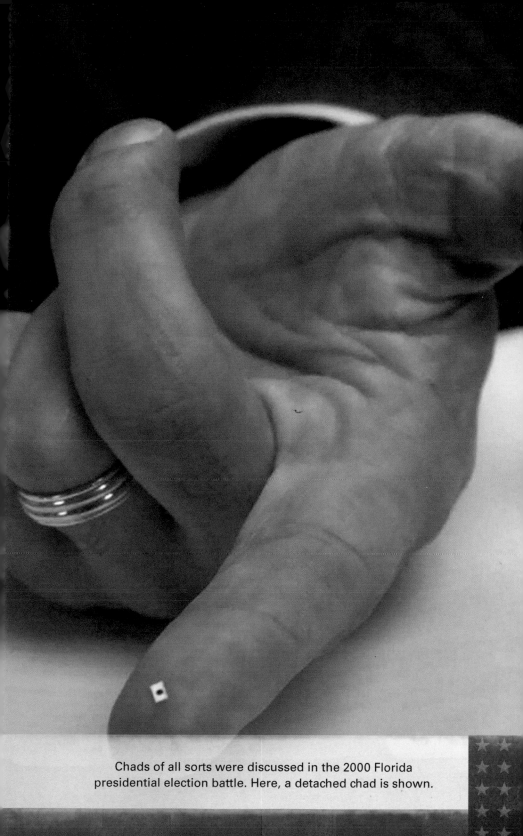

Chads of all sorts were discussed in the 2000 Florida presidential election battle. Here, a detached chad is shown.

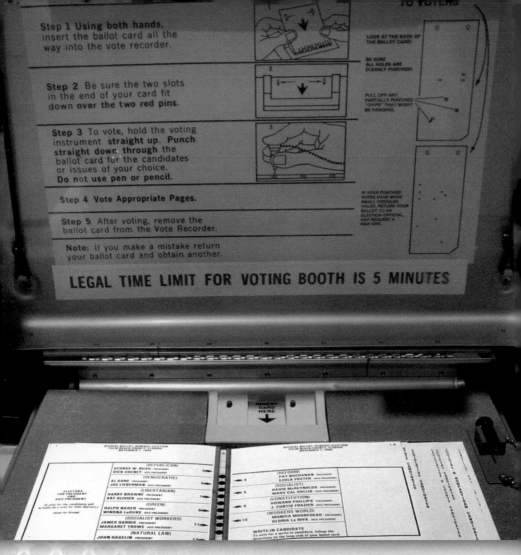

A Votomatic machine from Palm Beach County, Florida

Next, pressing the stylus against the perforated rectangle next to a candidate's name dislodges the rectangle—the chad—leaving a hole. As the voter turns the pages of the ballot booklet, new races and their corresponding rectangles are exposed. Finally, the punch card is inserted into a machine that reads it by passing light through the holes that have been punched.

But machines do not always operate as they are intended. If a Votomatic machine is old—many Florida precincts had used the same machines for decades—or not cleaned regularly, it becomes prone to error. Sometimes, issues result from human error. For example, if a voter does not press hard enough with the stylus, one or more chads may be left dangling from the ballot—hanging chads. When the ballot slides through the tabulation machine, the hanging chad can get pressed back into place. The machine's light cannot pass through the hole, making it seem as if no vote was made. As a result, a voter's choice for president or another office goes unrecorded.

For Gore and Bush, missing chads mattered most. A ballot on which the chad had cleanly detached from the punch card represented an obvious, clearly discernible vote.

Other Voting Concerns

Butterfly issues and hanging chads made many Americans question Florida's voting results. But these were not the only issues. Some voters simply did not follow directions. Voters were to select only one presidential candidate. Ballots indicating multiple presidential votes were deemed invalid. One voter in Bay County did not punch any holes. Instead, the voter wrote a note at the bottom of the ballot: "I forgot my glasses and cannot see this, please put Bush down for my vote."[11] Though he or she had clear intentions, the voter's ballot had to be discarded. Tabulation machines detect light, not handwritten pleas.

And then there were people who went to the polls on Election Day and were turned away. Some Floridians showed up at their polling places ready to cast their ballots, believing they had followed the voter registration procedure properly. But their names were

VOTER EDUCATION

Voter education is teaching people about voting. This includes informing citizens of their voting rights and election procedures, such as when, where, and how to vote. Simply put, it helps prepare voters to vote. Nonprofit organizations, including Nonprofit Vote and Rock the Vote, often carry out voter education. Such groups provide information in person, such as helping citizens register to vote, and via the Internet, with Web sites that have details and forms.

not on their precinct's list of registered voters. Some of these omissions resulted from clerical errors. A few years earlier, Florida had purged its lists in an attempt to remove ineligible voters, such as the deceased and convicted felons. Names of eligible voters may have been deleted in the process.

In addition, rumors of active discrimination, especially against African Americans, began to surface. Alarming stories appeared in the press about police erecting roadblocks in African-American neighborhoods to prevent people from reaching the polls.

Not all of the record number of African-American Floridians who turned out to vote in 2000—60 percent more than voted in the 1996 election—succeeded in doing so.[12] Bethune-Cookman College, a historically black college in Daytona Beach, had hosted on-campus voter-registration drives to encourage student turnout on Election Day. However, when some of the students showed up to vote, their names were not on the lists of registered voters. Also, voter education and voting equipment was more likely to be substandard in poorer districts, which tended to have substantial percentages of African-American voters, most of whom were Democrats. Such unequal conditions could have led

> If people do not know how to vote, it really does not matter what system you use or how technologically advanced it is. The key, in my view, is voter education, and until you get people learning how to vote and taking the act of voting seriously, you are never going to have accuracy."[13]
>
> —CHARLES BURTON, CHAIRMAN OF THE PALM BEACH COUNTY CANVASSING BOARD, IN A POSTELECTION INTERVIEW

to overvotes and undervotes—a ballot with no clear selection—that, it is reasonable to assume, would have gone for Gore.

Every election involves a certain amount of error, but one candidate usually wins by enough of a margin for voter errors to make no difference. A few thousand ineligible votes out of many millions cast do not affect the outcome unless the race is unbelievably close, which it was in the 2000 presidential race. On Thursday, November 9, the state of Florida released the unofficial results from its mandatory machine recount. Bush's lead had decreased dramatically from the 1,784 votes noted after Florida's polls closed. He was ahead by a mere 327 votes.[14]

Suddenly, all of the contested ballots—the undervotes, the overvotes, and the chads—mattered to Gore and the Democrats. Perhaps the machines read them wrong. Perhaps, upon closer inspection, some of those ballots would reveal clear preferences for one candidate or another and could be counted after all.

On the day Florida announced the results of the machine recount, the Florida Democratic Executive Committee filed requests for manual recounts in four heavily Democratic Florida counties: Palm Beach, Miami-Dade, Broward, and Volusia. The committee wanted the ballots evaluated by human beings instead of machines. Two days later, on November 11, Bush filed suit in federal district court in Miami to stop the recounts. The legal battle had begun. ～

Chapter 4

The Protest

When the possibility of a recount arises in an election, it is not hard to predict how the candidates will respond. The leading candidate will oppose a recount, wanting to hold on to the existing lead. The trailing candidate will favor a recount, hoping it will prove him or her the actual winner.

James A. Baker III, the chief legal adviser for Bush, counseled the Republicans not to ask for any recounts, even in solidly Republican counties where they stood a chance of picking up votes. Baker believed the Bush campaign should send a clear message: The election was over. Americans had chosen their president. And, it was time for Gore to accept the numbers and for Bush to get on with the business of preparing to run the country.

Gore did not want the fight over the election to drag on and try Americans' patience, but he felt compelled to press for accurate totals. Americans deserved assurance that the right man was going to Washington, even if the matter had to be settled in court. So he asked that votes be recounted in four counties. They were counties where he expected to gain votes. "Count every vote!" became the Gore team's mantra in the press, though the team did not want to recount votes in counties where Gore had the lead.[1]

Preparing for a Battle

Practically from the moment Gore retracted his concession, flocks of lawyers and political advisers descended on Tallahassee, Florida's capital, from around the state and the nation to offer their services. Both Bush and Gore chose lawyers who had experience in politics to lead their postelection strategy teams.

Baker headed the Republican side. He had extensive experience in politics and law. He was a longtime Bush family friend who hailed from Houston, Texas, where he was a senior partner at his family's law firm. Baker had served as secretary of the treasury under Reagan and secretary of state under George H. W. Bush. And

Katherine Harris, *left*, and James A. Baker were key players in Florida's historic recount case in 2000.

from 1976 to 1992, Baker had overseen five consecutive Republican presidential campaigns.

Warren Christopher headed Gore's team. He was a senior partner at a firm in Los Angeles, California. Christopher had served as secretary of state under Clinton and as deputy secretary of state under Jimmy Carter (1977–1981).

Baker convened the Bush group at Tallahassee's George H. W. Bush Center, the state's Republican Party headquarters. Christopher and the rest of the Gore crew hunkered down in rented retail space at a local strip mall. The candidates were not present. Bush was still in Texas, and Gore had left Nashville for Washington DC.

Neither side expected a clear path to victory. Christopher figured Florida's government would fight the Democrats at every turn, especially Republican governor Jeb Bush and Republican secretary of state Katherine Harris. The former was the presidential candidate's brother. The latter was responsible for certifying the vote totals.

Protest Filed

On November 9, Gore's attorneys asked for recounts in four counties: Palm Beach, Miami-Dade, Broward, and

SECRETARY OF STATE

Every US state has a secretary of state position, though a few states use the title secretary of the commonwealth or lieutenant governor. The responsibilities of the office vary from state to state and usually include overseeing state elections. In Florida, the office was defined by the state's constitution in 1838 and established in 1845. Initially, the role entailed maintaining Florida's public records and being the keeper of the state's seal, which made documents official. In 1969, the office expanded into the Florida Department of State and took on a variety of responsibilities. Today, Florida's secretary of state is head of the Department of State and chief of elections, as well as the chief cultural officer. Like the federal government, Florida's government has three branches. The executive branch implements and enforces laws, the judicial branch relates to justice or the courts, and the legislative branch makes laws. The secretary of state is part of the executive branch and does not have power over the courts, which are part of the judicial branch.

Volusia. The request was made as a **protest**, not filed as a **lawsuit**. Florida law states that any candidate or elector believing returns from an election are fraudulent or erroneous can protest those results within five days after the election or before the canvassing board adjourns, whichever happens last. Gore's team did not suggest anyone deliberately tampered with ballots but instead argued the margin of error with machine tabulation was too great for the original tallies to be relied upon in such a close race. The team wanted the ballots, especially the undervotes, held up to the light and examined by eyes, not computers. Eyes might be able to detect votes the machines missed. The four counties' canvassing boards had to decide whether their counties would comply with the protest and grant Gore's request.

As a first step, each county performed a sample manual recount of 1 percent of the presidential votes cast, a precursor required by Florida law to determine if a recount of all the county's votes appears justified. At the government center in Palm Beach, volunteers spread out across a row of approximately one dozen tables to diligently examine ballots, handing the trickier ones off to the three canvassing board members for further review. Even at this early stage, it was obvious a full recount would be a laborious, time-consuming, and exasperating process.

lawsuit—Legal action brought against a party.

protest—The legal method in Florida by which a voter or unsuccessful candidate in an election can challenge election returns before they are certified.

Theresa LePore, Palm Beach County election supervisor, examined a ballot during the county's manual recount.

Both parties had stationed representatives at the government center. They hovered over workers' shoulders, challenging votes found for the opposition. At times, the bickering became fierce. A rumor began circulating that Gore sympathizers were secretly

removing hanging chads and eating them to destroy
the evidence.

From the sample recounts, which were conducted
on November 11 and 12, Gore netted a small amount of
additional votes in each county, approximately 1 percent
of the number examined. The results seemed to indicate
enough error in the machine tabulation to make it likely
that manually recounting all votes in all four counties
would change the numbers at a potentially significant
level. With only a few hundred votes currently separating
the candidates, a handful of ballots awarded to Gore here
and there could add up to him gaining the lead.

But there was still much work to do, and questions
arose over whether such a monumental task could be
accomplished. Florida law required canvassing boards
to submit their tallies to Harris by Tuesday, November
14, one week after the election. Counties had only a
few days—Sunday, Monday, and part of Tuesday—
to go through hundreds of thousands of votes. They
had not even completely worked out the logistics for
the recount process. If the sample recount was any
indication, quibbling along party lines would slow down
the process considerably. Meeting the deadline would be
challenging, if not impossible.

Katherine Harris

Under everyday circumstances, the job of secretary of state in Florida is not especially conspicuous or glamorous. Yet Harris would emerge as a key player in the unfolding drama. The law gave her the power of certifying the state's returns, which essentially meant she had the power to end an election—in 2000, the presidential election. Once she officially certified the numbers, all debate over what counted as a vote and all the counting and recounting would stop, provided no legal action from voters or a candidate got it started again.

A Republican from a wealthy central Florida family, Harris was not well liked by the Democrats. They were wary because she had acted as a cochair for Bush's Florida campaign. As furor over recounts continued to rise, she drew criticism for everything from her apparent partisanship to her performances at press conferences to the way she applied her makeup. Even staunch Republicans could not deny she seemed firmly in their camp. And the Bush team took a step to ensure she stayed there by enlisting one of its own to act as her in-office adviser.

Republican Florida lobbyist and strategist Mac Stipanovich hurried to Harris's side to guide her and others in her office through the brewing controversy. His not-so-top-secret advice to her was to "bring the election in for a landing."[2] Thus, from the start, it was almost impossible to view Harris as impartial. Palm Beach Canvassing Board Chairman Charles Burton later observed, "I think it was clear that the secretary of state, Katherine Harris, would have certified the election on November 6 if she could have."[3]

The language pertaining to certification in the state's election law did leave ample room for confusion and debate. Florida **Statute** 102.111 stated,

> *If the county returns are not received by the Department of State by 5 p.m. of the seventh day following an election, all missing counties shall be ignored, and the results shown by the returns on file shall be certified.*[4]

But a later section of the statute changes the wording slightly, substituting "may be ignored" for "shall be ignored."[5] That one little word, *may*, implied Harris

---

statute—A law put into effect by the legislative branch of government.

had a choice. She could ignore late returns, but she did not have to. If she decided to follow the second part of the statute rather than the first, she had the option of giving the counties the time they needed to conduct recounts—or she could cut them off before they even started. Any haggling over deadlines would not matter, however, if a lawsuit Bush wanted to pursue succeeded.

First Court Appearance

On November 13, in a packed Miami courtroom, US District Court Judge Donald M. Middlebrooks listened to Bush lawyer Ted Olson argue that the hand recounts Gore had asked for were subjective and unfair. Florida law did not set a uniform standard for recount procedures, so it was possible that different counties would evaluate ballots differently. That is, the counties would treat votes unequally. This, Olson contended, made the recounts **unconstitutional** under the equal protection clause of the Fourteenth Amendment. Olson claimed additional unfairness in Gore's

> " This is the type of case where there are very, very serious issues. We think that the [manual recount] system is fundamentally flawed because it counts different votes differently in different parts of the state."[6]
>
> —TED OLSON, BUSH ATTORNEY, NOVEMBER 13, 2000

selective choice of counties. If Gore truly cared about counting every vote, he would have requested recounts in all 67 Florida counties, not just the four most likely to slant Democrat. Gore's lead lawyer, Laurence Tribe, countered by noting that questions such as these were for the state, not a federal district court, to decide and that recounts had been standard procedure in close elections throughout Florida history without anyone raising a fuss.

Middlebrooks ruled on the case that day. Agreeing with Tribe, the judge said,

> The procedures employed by Florida appear to be neutral and, while not yet complete, the process seems to be unfolding as it has on other occasions. . . . I believe that intervention by a

> " The electoral process is a balance between the desire of each individual voter to have his or her intended vote recorded and the right of the public to a clear, final result within a reasonable time. We are trying to bring the election in for a landing. We think a process that has no end is a disservice to everyone who cast a ballot in this election."[7]
>
> —*KATHERINE HARRIS, FLORIDA SECRETARY OF STATE, NOVEMBER 13, 2000*

unconstitutional—Inconsistent with a constitution.

THE FOURTEENTH AMENDMENT

Congress ratified the Fourteenth Amendment in 1868. The Thirteenth Amendment had abolished slavery in 1865. Soon after, many Southern states passed discriminatory laws that restricted black people's civil liberties, barring them from voting, gathering in groups, and other freedoms whites enjoyed. The Fourteenth Amendment gave blacks citizenship, guaranteed "equal protection of the laws," and promised due process of law, meaning that no one could deny them life, liberty, or property except under a just application of the legal process.[9] Section 1 of the amendment states,

> All persons born or naturalized in the United States . . . are citizens of the United States and of the State wherein they reside. No State shall make or enforce any law which shall abridge the privileges or immunities of citizens of the United States; nor shall any State deprive any person of life, liberty, or property, without due process of law; nor deny to any person within its [territory] the equal protection of the laws.[10]

Among other things, this amendment aims to enforce the idea that people are created equal and states must treat them equally.

federal district court, particularly on a preliminary basis, is inappropriate."[8]

He also dismissed Bush's charge that recounts violated his **constitutional** rights as a candidate.

Gore and his attorneys could savor their victory in this particular battle, though not for long. If Harris went ahead with her plan to certify Florida's results on the evening of November 14, before the counties finished recounting, Democrats would have to take further legal action to keep alive Gore's chances of becoming president.

Indecision had stalled the proceedings in three of the four counties. Only Volusia, the smallest in the group with 179,661 ballots, persisted with recounting while awaiting the court's decision.[11] It would manage to finish five minutes before the deadline. Gore picked up 27 votes in Volusia, which dropped Bush's statewide lead to 300.[12] As the hour of certification loomed, Miami-Dade decided against doing a recount. Broward and Palm Beach still planned to recount but were bogged down in logistics. Florida law did not allow for recounting only undervotes—the counties had to do all or none. In Palm Beach alone, 462,587 votes awaited scrutiny.[13] The canvassing board members' only hope to complete a recount was for Harris to agree to extend the deadline—or for a court to order her to do so. ∼

constitutional—In accordance with a constitution.

Stopping Harris

As the Palm Beach Canvassing Board waited for Harris's decision about extending the recount deadline, it received advice on conducting a recount. Kerey Carpenter, a Republican lawyer from Harris's office who was in Palm Beach to report on the situation, recommended that Burton, the board's chairman, send a message to Harris asking for an **advisory opinion**. He did. Director of the Florida Division of Elections Clay Roberts, who reported to Harris, advised the board that it should not authorize a manual recount unless the members found

advisory opinion—An opinion issued by a court or government official that is not legally binding but offers advice on constitutionality or interpretation of a law.

Katherine Harris drew criticism for her efforts to certify election results quickly.

discrepancies "caused by incorrect election parameters or software error."[1] This opinion favored Bush.

Another state official offered an opposing opinion—one that favored Gore. Florida Attorney General Bob Butterworth, a Democrat, gave the board his own advisory opinion. The state's chief legal officer said hand recounts were permissible if the election result was in doubt. But these were not official rulings, which were what the canvassing board really needed from Harris.

Be Reasonable

On November 14, one week after Election Day, the new US president still had not been officially declared. That day, Leon County Circuit Court Judge Terry P. Lewis had to decide whether Gore had legal justification for preventing Harris from certifying on November 14 as she had planned.

Lewis's ruling in Tallahassee that afternoon gave a slight boost to Gore and the canvassing boards, but he handed them a blow as well. He upheld the 5:00 p.m., November 14, certification deadline and also directed Harris to be reasonable. Lewis said Harris could not arbitrarily ignore late returns. Harris must instead use her "discretion," giving thoughtful consideration to and articulating sound reasons as to why she would or would not accept them.[3]

The judge advised any county unable to meet the deadline to write a letter to Harris stating why more time was needed, and, under Lewis's order, Harris could

> " Ultimately what we wound up realizing is that everybody up the chain was acting very partisan"[4]
>
> —CHARLES BURTON, PALM BEACH COUNTY CANVASSING BOARD CHAIRMAN, REGARDING THE ADVISORY OPINIONS THE BOARD RECEIVED

not reject these counties outright. She had to offer a reasonable argument for her decision.

In part, the Palm Beach County Canvassing Board had dallied going forward with a recount because members were not completely sure a recount was legally permissible. The wording of Florida election law said canvassing boards should opt to recount if they suspected "an error in vote tabulation which could affect the outcome of the election."[5] What constituted an error was unclear.

Democrats advocated a broader definition. Errors included situations in which ballots that should have been tabulated were not run through the machine correctly or were otherwise mistakenly discounted. Republicans supported a stricter definition: a more sweeping mechanical failure, such as faulty computer software, which could cause tabulation machines to malfunction at the time of the count. Under the more rigid interpretation of the law, conditions for recounts in the four counties had not been met.

As the battle between the major political parties took place in the Palm Beach County Government Center, partisan behavior was on full display outside the building. Supporters for Gore and Bush chanted, jeered at one another, and waved signs. Gore demonstrators called for a revote and denounced LePore's butterfly ballot as the Bush crowd heckled the Democrats for being "too dumb to read" instructions.[6]

Harris's Decision

On November 14, Harris made her decision regarding the recount deadline: it would not be extended. Volusia had finished its recount, so her decision would affect the three remaining counties: Broward, Miami-Dade, and Palm Beach. To comply with the judge's order, however, Harris gave the counties with late returns until 2:00 p.m. the next day to explain in writing why they should be allowed more time. The counties complied with her

LEPORE'S EXPERIENCE

In the days following the 2000 presidential election, media descended upon the Palm Beach Government Center from around the world. When members of Palm Beach's canvassing board went to talk to the swarm of reporters, they did so surrounded by sheriff's deputies and a SWAT team for protection. Board member LePore, approver of the butterfly ballot, noted, "They got around me, literally, practically carried me through, and people were pulling at me, calling me names, screaming at me."[7]

For weeks after the election, LePore received boxes of mail. Some of it was complimentary and sympathetic to her predicament. Some of the mail was hateful and accusatory. Television cameras followed her everywhere, an extremely unwelcome development for someone used to—and most comfortable with—working behind the scenes. Overworked and overstressed, she ended up losing 22 pounds (10 kg).[8]

request but to no avail. Though she had not yet certified the results, on November 15, Harris dismissed the counties' reasoning and denied them the opportunity to submit amended tallies.

> " Shortly after the results are known, we should both come together for another meeting, to reaffirm our national unity. If I turn out to be successful, I'll be ready to travel to Governor Bush's home. If I am not, I'll be ready to meet him wherever he wishes."[11]
>
> —AL GORE, NOVEMBER 15, 2000

The day had been marked by exchanges between the candidates. Gore announced on television that evening, "We need a resolution that is fair and final. We need to move expeditiously to the most complete and accurate count that is possible."[9] Bush replied to Gore a few hours later in his own televised announcement:

> *The outcome of this election will not be the result of deals or efforts to mold public opinion. The outcome of this election will be determined by the votes and by the law.*[10]

But these were not the only announcements related to the Florida election issued that day. Between Gore's and Bush's statements, Harris proclaimed in

Tallahassee that she was going to certify the results received from Florida's county canvassing boards by the coming Tuesday. Harris said, "The reasons given in the requests are insufficient to warrant waiver of the unambiguous filing deadline imposed by the Florida Legislature."[12] Judge Lewis had told Harris to use her discretion in interpreting the law, and Harris believed she had done so.

> "Once this election is over, I would be glad to meet with Vice President Gore, and I join him in pledging that regardless of who wins after this weekend's final count, we will work together to unite our great country."[13]
> —GEORGE W. BUSH, NOVEMBER 15, 2000

The Democrats did not agree. They thought Harris had acted for no other reason than to get Bush into office. Gore would have to return to the courts for another ruling. ～

Chapter 6

Going to the Florida Supreme Court

*H*arris's decision not to extend the recount deadline for Broward, Miami-Dade, and Palm Beach Counties did not resolve the election issue. In an attempt to get Harris's certification invalidated, Gore's team filed a **motion** and immediately sought an emergency ruling from Judge Lewis on whether Harris had ignored his earlier instructions.

motion—A formal proposal to a court or judge asking for an order, ruling, or direction.

Bush supporters protested outside the Florida Supreme Court on November 15, 2000.

Lewis Rules Again

Lewis heard the case, called *McDermott v. Harris*, on November 16. Michael McDermott was a member of the Volusia County Canvassing Board. Gore was also named among the **plaintiffs**. Dexter Douglass, the lead Florida lawyer for Gore, argued that Harris had given the counties contradictory information. First, she told them the recounts were not legally justified. After they stopped counting, she told the counties she would not accept the new numbers because the deadline had passed. Douglass likened this to a police officer stopping a driver, which causes a backup of cars, and then issuing a ticket to the driver for blocking traffic. In other words, it was a no-win situation for the counties.

The judge did not agree. On November 17, in a one-page ruling, Lewis wrote,

> *On the limited evidence presented, it appears that the Secretary has exercised her reasoned judgment to determine what relevant factors and criteria should be considered, applied them to the facts and circumstances pertinent to the individual counties involved, and made her decision.*[1]

That same day, November 17, Gore's team filed an **appeal**. The state's First District **Court of Appeal** asked the Florida Supreme Court to take the case, relieving the district court of it. Florida law granted the district court this right. Despite having a packed calendar, the state supreme court agreed to the request and made hearing the case a priority. In addition, the court instructed Harris and her office not to certify election results until it ruled on the case.

appeal—To petition a higher court to review the decision or proceedings of a lower court.

court of appeal—A court that hears cases appealed from the trial courts in its district.

plaintiff—The person or group who initiates a lawsuit.

Absentee Ballots

Harris had not certified the election results on the state's November 14 deadline. Besides the issues surrounding the recount, there were other votes still missing. Harris was waiting for outstanding absentee ballots—mail-in votes cast primarily by men and women who were out of the country on Election Day. Due in Harris's office by November 17, many of these votes came from military personnel, a group tending to vote Republican. The general consensus was that the absentee votes would increase Bush's lead—and they did. These ballots added to the controversy.

> " The campaign is over, but a test of our democracy is now under way. It is a test we must pass. And it is a test we will pass with flying colors. All we need is a common agreement that what is at stake here is not who wins and who loses in a contest for the presidency, but how we honor our Constitution and make sure that our democracy works as our founders intended it to work. This is a time to respect every voter and every vote."[3]
>
> —AL GORE, NOVEMBER 15, 2000

Election law required these votes to be signed or postmarked no later than November 7, Election Day, to count. And this became a point of dispute. Theoretically, any vote postmarked after that date or arriving with no postmark date would be disregarded. However, Harris instructed canvassing boards to accept any vote signed and dated on November 7, even if postmarked the following day. Since the law stipulated that absentee votes needed to be signed or postmarked no later than Election Day, that means a vote postmarked November 8 or later but signed November 7 or earlier could be accepted. Democrats accused Republicans of trying to round up as many votes as they could by counting votes that were clearly invalid. Republicans charged Democrats with wanting to unfairly penalize absentee voters.

ABSENTEE VOTING

Absentee voting has been part of US history since colonial times. In 1635, the Massachusetts Bay Colony allowed some residents to stay behind and guard their towns on Election Day. These voters sent their sealed votes to Boston with their colleagues. The American Civil War (1861–1865) and World War I (1914–1918) saw increased interest in absentee voting so soldiers could cast ballots while away on duty. The custom became further entrenched during World War II (1941–1945). In recent decades, absentee voting requirements have been relaxed to allow a far greater number of voters to vote without entering a polling place, thus increasing voter participation.

THE FLORIDA SUPREME COURT

Florida's supreme court was established in 1845 when Florida became a US state. The court began hearing arguments the following year. Initially, the court did not have its own justices. Rather, judges from Florida's trial courts served in this capacity. There were four circuits of trial courts, which resulted in a maximum of four justices on the supreme court. This changed in 1851, when the state's constitution was amended to provide the court with its own justices: one chief justice and two associate justices. The number of justices has fluctuated, increasing to six, and then changing to five, six, and then seven, which is the current number.

The selection of justices has varied, too. At first, the state legislature elected justices, and then the people did. Later, the governor appointed them, with the Senate's input and approval.

Since its inception, the court has had more than 80 justices serve in its ranks. In 2000, the court consisted of five men and two women: Harry Lee Anstead, Major B. Harding, R. Fred Lewis, Barbara J. Pariente, Leander J. Shaw Jr., Peggy A. Quince, and Charles T. Wells.

Because so many of the absentee ballots came from the military, some critics saw Gore's questioning of them as unpatriotic. Gore's running mate, Joe Lieberman, went on national television to answer these charges. In an appearance on the NBC Sunday morning news show *Meet the Press*, Lieberman attempted to reassure viewers:

> Let me just say that the vice president and I would never authorize, and would not tolerate, a campaign that was aimed specifically at invalidating absentee ballots from members of our armed services.[4]

Instead, he said, they advocated giving military ballots "the benefit of the doubt."[5] Gore's team did not aggressively challenge Florida's absentee ballots.

Florida's Supreme Court

Though the Democrats did not pursue the absentee ballots, the case against Harris remained. It was scheduled to go before the Florida Supreme Court on November 20. Many observers felt the Democrats had reason for optimism. All seven **justices**—five men, two women—had been appointed by Democratic governors. In addition, the court had repeatedly sided against Governor Jeb Bush and the Republican

chief justice—The presiding judge of a court.

justice—A member of a supreme court.

preside—To hear and oversee a legal proceeding.

On November 21, 2000, Thomas D. Hall, clerk of the Florida Supreme Court, looked over the petitions filed with the court since November 15.

legislature in recent history. Jeb Bush publicly admitted to the existence of "a little bit of tension" between his administration and the court, over which **Chief Justice** Charles T. Wells **presided**.[6] However, the governor also expressed faith that the justices would not allow politics to get in the way of doing their job in the recount suit.

Television cameras had been closely following the actions of the Florida courts and canvassing boards, and this appeal, *Palm Beach County Canvassing Board v. Harris*, would be no different. The appeal consolidated several legal actions, including *McDermott v. Harris*. The legal **briefs**, opinions, and transcripts of court proceedings had been published online, so people near and far could follow along by reading as well.

On November 21, two weeks after the election, the court announced its unanimous decision: Harris had disenfranchised Florida voters by failing to use her discretion. The recounts should continue.

The justices wrote in their **per curiam opinion** that their goal was "to reach the result that reflects the will of the voters, whatever that may be."[7] The justices rejected Harris's claim that the law allowed for recounts only in situations of total mechanical system failure:

> *Although error cannot be completely eliminated in any tabulation of the ballots, our society has not yet gone so far as to place blind faith in machines. In*

brief—A document that establishes the legal argument of a case.

per curiam opinion—An opinion issued by the entire court as a whole, not attributed to any single judge.

Judge Charles Burton, *front*, Palm Beach County Canvassing Board chair, watched a broadcast of the Florida Supreme Court's recount ruling on November 21, 2000.

almost all endeavors, including elections, humans routinely correct the errors of machines.[8]

As far as the court was concerned, humans had every legal right to correct those errors in this election. At the close of their opinion, the justices set a new certification time and date: 5:00 p.m. on Sunday, November 26, 2000, or, if Harris's office was not open on Sunday, 9:00 a.m. on Monday, November 27.

The justices did not explain how they determined the new certification date. To many, especially outraged Republicans, the selection of November 26 seemed arbitrary. Others questioned if the court had upheld Florida's constitution or if it had crossed into legislative territory and begun making new law. Bush's team was furious at the Florida Supreme Court for changing voting rules in the middle of the election process—they felt the ruling violated the state's constitution, which set forth the powers of the legislature, not the court, to decide how electors are chosen. The Bush team wanted this uncertainty to be answered by the nation's highest court: the US Supreme Court. ～

Chapter 7

Bush v. Palm Beach County Canvassing Board

*E*very year, the US Supreme Court receives approximately 10,000 **petitions** for **writs of certiorari**, of which it hears arguments in 75 to 80 cases. The US Supreme Court is the highest court in the land, so once it decides a case, there is no higher

petition—A formal written request to a court requesting action on a particular matter.

writ of certiorari—An order from a higher court to a lower court calling for the record of a case for review.

court to appeal to. There are no more appeals, no other courts from which to seek an alternate opinion.

Bush's Writ of Certiorari

Bush filed a petition for a writ of certiorari on November 22, the day after the Florida Supreme Court handed down its opinion. In the petition, Bush's team argued that the Florida Supreme Court's ruling to extend the recount deadline led to three federal violations. First, Florida's justices defied Title 3, Section 5 of the US election code by changing state election law after the voting had taken place. Second, the Florida decision went against Article II of the US Constitution, which specifies that state legislatures, not state courts, have the ultimate authority to choose presidential electors. Third, the recount subjected Bush to unfair treatment under the Fourteenth Amendment's equal protection clause.

Bush's lawyers requested in a written motion that the justices speed up their normal deliberation schedule. Members of the Electoral College would cast their votes on December 18, so time was of the essence. Lead Bush lawyer Ted Olson asked for the deadline for submission of briefs from both sides to be November 24, with an argument date of December 5. Not only did the justices grant a writ of certiorari, which meant they would take the case, they proposed an even swifter pace. They would hear **oral arguments** for the case on December 1. But they agreed to consider only two of Bush's three claims—those pertaining to Title 3 and Article II.

For the US Supreme Court to take a case, at least four of the nine justices must vote to grant a petition. When Bush's appeal arrived at the court building, most justices were already out for the Thanksgiving holiday, but their clerks tracked them down and rushed the

ARTICLE II, SECTION 1, CLAUSE 2

Article II, Section 1, Clause 2 of the Constitution regards appointment of electors to the Electoral College and states,

Each State shall appoint, in such Manner as the Legislature thereof may direct, a Number of Electors, equal to the whole Number of Senators and Representatives to which the State may be entitled in the Congress: but no Senator or Representative, or Person holding an Office of Trust or Profit under the United States, shall be appointed an Elector.[1]

Bush's argument interpreted this clause as saying state legislatures have the ultimate authority to choose electors. In effect, this interpretation means the state legislatures make rules for how votes are counted and courts cannot interfere with that authority.

WHEN THE ELECTORAL COLLEGE VOTES

Article II, Section 1 of the US Constitution addresses when the Electoral College will vote:

> The Congress may determine the Time of choosing the Electors, and the Day on which they shall give their Votes; which Day shall be the same throughout the United States.[2]

Title 3, Chapter 1, Section 7 of US legal code further details the voting day:

> The electors of President and Vice President of each State shall meet and give their votes on the first Monday after the second Wednesday in December next following their appointment at such place in each State as the legislature of such State shall direct.[3]

Republican briefs into their hands. Justice Anthony Kennedy, who oversees preliminary matters on appeals coming in from the Eleventh Circuit, which includes Florida, tallied his colleagues' votes on Thanksgiving Day and the next morning: five to grant; four to deny. William Rehnquist, Sandra Day O'Connor, Antonin Scalia, Anthony Kennedy, and Clarence Thomas voted

oral argument—A spoken presentation of a legal case by a lawyer.

to take the case. John Paul Stevens, David Souter, Ruth Bader Ginsburg, and Stephen Breyer voted to deny the petition and not take the case.

Recount Status

As both sides prepared to give their oral arguments in the nation's highest court, recounts continued in Florida—at least in two counties. Volusia had met the first deadline, and Miami-Dade decided to halt its recount on November 22. Palm Beach and Broward Counties remained. They based their actions on the ruling made by the state supreme court. But only some of the votes were recounted, and even fewer were accepted by Harris.

At approximately 7:30 p.m. on Sunday, November 26, the deadline set by the state supreme court, Harris appeared on television to declare Bush the winner in Florida. She had certified the results.

Broward County had completed its recount, which added 567 votes to Gore's total, but that was not enough to give him the lead. Bush had 2,912,790 votes and Gore had 2,912,253: Bush won by 537 votes.[4]

Miami-Dade, partly in response to pressure from Republican protesters, had ceased its recount. Palm Beach pressed Harris for a few more hours,

Judge Robert Rosenberg of the Broward County Canvassing
Board examined a ballot on November 24, 2000.

Harris certified Florida's presidential election results on November 26, 2000, declaring Bush the winner. Her official act did not resolve the recount issue.

assuring her the recount would finish by the 9:00 a.m. Monday secondary deadline the Florida court had suggested. The secretary of state denied the request. Palm Beach submitted the tallies from its partial recount, planning to finish examining the last 1,000 ballots that evening with the hope that amended returns might be accepted at a later time. Harris rejected the partial-recount totals and used the same Palm Beach numbers she had included in the November 14 certification.

Although Harris certified Bush the winner, she did not settle the recount issue. Bush's and Gore's teams pressed on with preparing for the US Supreme Court. In a matter of days, they would make their cases in Washington DC.

The Oral Arguments

On December 1, the US Supreme Court courtroom was packed. Bush's team argued first. Olson was interrupted by justices almost immediately. "We're looking for a federal issue," Kennedy stated.[5] O'Connor elaborated, saying,

> *If it were purely a matter of state law, I suppose we normally would leave it alone, where the state supreme court found it, and so you probably have to persuade us there's some issue of federal law here.*[6]

THE 2000 US SUPREME COURT

In order of seniority, the US Supreme Court justices who heard and decided *Bush v. Gore* in 2000 were William Rehnquist, appointed in 1972 and made chief justice in 1986; John Paul Stevens, 1975; Sandra Day O'Connor, 1981; Antonin Scalia, 1986; Anthony Kennedy, 1988; David Souter, 1990; Clarence Thomas, 1991; Ruth Bader Ginsburg, 1993; and Stephen Breyer, 1994.

A little later, Ginsburg admonished Olson, noting, "I do not know of any case where we have [challenged] a state supreme court the way you are doing in this case."[7] The justices needed to be persuaded that the case belonged within their **jurisdiction** rather than the state of Florida's.

The line of questioning appeared favorable to Gore at the start of the session, and then the tone shifted. Rehnquist and Scalia bombarded Gore lawyer Laurence Tribe with questions during his arguments. Scalia asked, "What makes you think the Florida Legislature affirmatively invited the Florida Supreme Court?"[8] Scalia meant that, according to Article II of the Constitution, it was the business of the legislature to determine electors and the court had no right to change the rules. Tribe maintained that since the laws were "self-contradictory," the Florida Supreme Court had the authority to determine what lawmakers had meant, and the court had acted in the interest of the voters.[9]

Deliberation

After the US Supreme Court justices finished hearing oral arguments on December 1, they entered their conference room for deliberation that afternoon.

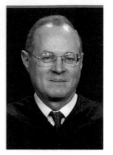

EPHEN
REYER

SANDRA DAY
O'CONNOR

RUTH BADER
GINSBURG

ANTHONY
KENNEDY

VILLIAM
HNQUIST

ANTONIN
SCALIA

DAVID
SOUTER

JOHN PAUL
STEVENS

CLARENCE
THOMAS

The justices of the 2000 US Supreme Court

Although the proceedings in the courtroom had been recorded—not on camera, but on audiotape—and would be released to the public later that day, discussion in the conference room is always off the record.

jurisdiction—The authority to govern or try cases; also refers to the territory under that authority.

Released on Monday, December 4, the opinion in *Bush v. Palm Beach County Canvassing Board* was relatively brief and issued per curiam. The justices explained they still were not clear on the reasoning behind the Florida Supreme Court's decision. And not knowing the "precise grounds" was, in their view,

THE DELIBERATION PROCESS

US Supreme Court tradition dictates a certain pattern to the justices' conversations in their private meeting to determine whether to take on a case. "We are fairly rigid in our rules: We talk in the order of seniority about the case," Stevens explained.[10] They do not interrupt one another in midsentence or speak out of turn. The chief justice always speaks first, followed by the justice who has been on the court the longest, and so on down the line until the most recently appointed member has voiced his or her views. If further discussion is needed, they go around the table again in the same order.

Often, once a decision is reached, the chief justice, if he or she is in the majority, assigns the authoring of the ruling to one of the justices. A unanimous opinion means all nine justices voted the same way, and any of them could potentially write the opinion. If the opinion is not unanimous, the senior-most justice gives the task to a justice in the majority, while justices in the minority have the option of crafting dissents, which are official written statements that disagree with the majority decision.

"sufficient reason for us to decline at this time to review the federal questions asserted to be present."[11] In other words, they had decided not to decide, and they sent the case back to the Florida Supreme Court. They **vacated** the judgment of the Florida Supreme Court, which now had to issue a new decision—one that included an explanation.

The court's ruling did not settle the matter or decide the 2000 race for president. Instead, the battle over Florida returned to Florida and moved into a new phase. Protesting was over. Contesting would begin. ～

vacate—To make legally void.

Chapter 8

The Contest

*U*ntil Harris certified Florida's election results on November 26, Gore's push for recounts in the four Florida counties was a protest under Florida election law. Any lawsuits he filed after certification would be a contest of the certification—an expanded objection from the four counties to the entire state. A contest occurs when the losing candidate argues that, in the words of Florida's election code, "certain acts occurred sufficient to have affected the result."[1]

In the suit *Gore v. Harris*, which Gore's team hurried to file in Leon County on November 27, the "acts" involved thousands of allegedly uncounted, miscounted, or counted-but-not-included ballots in Miami-Dade, Palm Beach, and Nassau Counties. In a legal sense, Gore now would have to consider

Gore's recount slogan, "Count Every Vote," became the mantra for many Floridians as well.

the county canvassing boards foes instead of friends. He would have to list them as **defendants**, along with Harris, in a suit filed with the hope the courts—initially the Leon County Circuit Court, but this was clearly going to a higher court for review—would order the canvassing boards to resume recounting and submit votes Harris had previously disallowed.

Sometimes, those votes were 100 or so here and a few dozen there. In Nassau County, for instance, the automatic machine recount had produced a total lower than the original number of votes, while at the same time recording 51 new votes for Gore. The county canvassing board submitted the original returns to Harris. Gore argued that the new tally was the one that should have been certified.

Other Absentee Ballot Battles

As the opposing teams worked to settle the matter of Florida's 2000 presidential election results, another battle over absentee ballots was unfolding, separately from the contest, in the largely Republican counties of Seminole and Martin. It was a battle in which Gore decided not to participate.

Questioning the validity of absentee ballots still presented a thorny issue for the candidate. Not only did Gore not want to appear antimilitary, but his stance on recounts—count every vote—would be difficult to reconcile with a lawsuit that, if successful, would lead to discarding thousands of ballots. Other Democrats stepped in and took on the issue. Harry Jacobs, a Florida lawyer unaffiliated with Gore's legal team, had discovered improper handling of some absentee ballots in Seminole County. He refused to keep silent on the matter.

While working as a volunteer to help oversee Seminole County's automatic machine recount mandated by the state law in close elections, Jacobs heard an election worker talking to a canvassing board member about how, before the election, Republican volunteers had "corrected" misprinted absentee ballot applications that mistakenly did not include a required identification number.[2] The more Jacobs found out about the situation, the more he believed the corrections volunteers added to more than 4,500 applications were technically illegal.[3]

defendant—The person against whom legal action is brought.

GORE'S REASONS FOR FIGHTING

In a November 26 interview with a reporter from the *New York Times*, Gore explained his reasons for continuing to fight:

> *I think that it is important for the integrity of our democracy to make sure that every vote is counted. Especially in a close election because the foundation of our constitutional self-government is the consent of the governed . . . it is a relatively simple principle that lies at the heart of our democracy that every vote that is legally cast must be fairly and accurately counted in accordance with the law.*[4]

It is important to remember that Gore asked for a recount in only four of Florida's 67 counties. One could argue that this contradicts his explanation and that his belief in the idea that every vote is counted would mean that Gore would have sought a recount in every county.

Although many absentee ballots come from overseas, others are submitted by voters in the United States who, for one reason or another, cannot or do not want to visit their polling places on Election Day. A voter must apply to receive an absentee ballot. It had become standard practice for both Democrat and Republican campaign offices to mail applications to party members weeks before Election Day in an effort to increase voter response. Once a voter signs, dates, and returns an application, it is a legal document and cannot be altered. But for the 2000 election, Republican volunteers in Seminole and Martin Counties added missing voter identification numbers to a few thousand signed absentee ballots. The error was the result of the printer, not the voters. Republicans reasoned that voters—and Bush—should not suffer by having the ballots rejected for what seemed like a minor technicality.

What was not so minor was how the discarding of these ballots could potentially affect the outcome of the election. Because votes are cast anonymously, there was no way of telling postelection which ones came from the altered applications. In *Jacobs v. Seminole County Canvassing Board*, Jacobs sought to have all of the county's 15,215 absentee ballots—10,006 for Bush and 5,209 for Gore—thrown out.[5]

In a separate but similar suit, *Taylor v. Martin County Canvassing Board*, Democrat Ronald Taylor asked for all 9,773 absentee ballots in Martin County—6,294 for Bush and 3,349 for Gore—to be discarded.[6] Harris had certified the election on November 26 with a 537-vote margin in favor of Bush. Victories for Jacobs and Taylor could mean that, instead of Gore losing by hundreds of votes, he would have won by thousands.

Oral arguments for both cases began on the same day, December 6, in adjacent courtrooms at the Leon County Courthouse in Tallahassee, away from the activity of the recount. They were heard by Judge Terry Lewis, who had ruled in the previous circuit court recount cases, and Judge Nikki Ann Clark. Both judges ruled in the Republicans' favor. The two believed the counties had acted counter to election law but deemed that tampering with ballot applications was less of an offense than altering actual ballots. In their written opinions, the judges scolded the county canvassing boards but decided their actions, in Lewis's words, "were not egregious enough to warrant the extreme remedy of

A NINE-VOTE WIN

At one point, Gore's lawyers deduced that if the recounts he asked for in *Gore v. Harris* went forward, the vice president could win the election in Florida by 9 votes. The equation proposed by Gore's team was 215 votes from the prematurely stopped Palm Beach County recount plus 157 votes from Miami-Dade County evaluated before they halted their recount, plus 51 votes from Nassau County found during the mandatory machine recount, plus 123 invalid absentee votes subtracted from Bush's total of 537 equals Gore wins by 9 votes. The math would have been different if the state supreme court had ruled to count everything.[7]

disqualifying all the absentee ballots and thwarting the will of the people."[8]

Gore's hope of gaining enough votes to overtake Bush lay in one place only: the contest suit. And time was running out.

Gore v. Harris

Opening arguments in *Gore v. Harris*, Gore's contest suit, began December 2, 2000. Judge N. Sanders Sauls's courtroom was packed with an audience of reporters, news photographers, and other spectators. Bush's lead lawyer, Barry Richard, accused Gore of unfair play. He claimed Gore's request for recounts was akin to demanding "three free shots at the basket."[9]

Gore's attorneys did not consider the recounts as a do-over but as a do-it-right—a chance to correct errors that were made the first time around. They spent much of the day trying to prove that faulty equipment prevented some voters from fully punching their cards. They called a voting machine specialist to the stand to testify on how easily a machine with worn-out parts or a collection area clogged with chads could keep the stylus from going all the way through the paper. From the Gore team's perspective, dimpled chads clearly indicated voter intent. Head Gore lawyer David Boies argued that the dimpled chads should be counted: "There is sufficient evidence that those votes could change or at least place in doubt the results of the election."[10]

Arguments went on for two days. A reporter for the *New York Times* wrote, after a particularly belabored second day of testimony, that Gore's "twin foes" were "now George W. Bush and the calendar."[11]

But on December 4, the same day the US Supreme Court sent *Bush v. Palm Beach County Canvassing Board* back to Florida for review, Judge Sauls issued his ruling in *Gore v. Harris*. It was a resounding defeat for Gore. Citing the 1982 case *Smith v. Tynes* as a **precedent**, Sauls declared that Gore's lawyers had failed to show a "reasonable probability," not just a "reasonable possibility," that recounting the disputed ballots would result in him winning the election.[12] Sauls found that the Palm Beach County Canvassing Board had used its discretion—"which no court may overrule absent a clear abuse of discretion"—in rejecting the 3,300 undervotes Gore wanted reevaluated.[13] Overall, Sauls

precedent—A court ruling or decision that becomes an example and is noted in later rulings in similar cases.

Members of the Florida Supreme Court prepared to hear oral arguments in the Florida election ballot recount case on December 7, 2000.

summarized in his written opinion, which he read aloud in the courtroom, "The court finds and concludes the evidence does not establish any illegality, dishonesty, gross negligence, improper influence, coercion, or fraud in the balloting and counting processes."[14] All of Gore's requests were denied.

Another Appeal

Before the day was over, Gore's legal team appealed Sauls's decision to the Florida Supreme Court. A little more than two weeks earlier, that court had ruled to honor voter intent in the 2000 presidential election in

Gore attorney David Boies presented his oral argument in the recount case to the Florida Supreme Court on December 7, 2000.

Florida. The Democrats' now-desperate hope was that they would do so again.

The Florida Supreme Court heard arguments in *Gore v. Harris* on December 7. The court ruled on the case December 8. In a 4–3 decision, it overturned Sauls's ruling and called for manual recounts of undervotes in the entire state.

If the Republicans thought it unfair for Gore to request recounts in four heavily Democratic counties, then one reasonable solution would be to examine the 60,000 or so undervotes in the other 63 counties, too.[15] And, as the justices said, "Because time is of the essence, the recount shall commence immediately."[16] Bush sent an emergency request to the US Supreme Court that the Florida Supreme Court's action be stopped. Bush's request initiated the *Bush v. Gore* case.

Recount Standards

Meanwhile, Judge Lewis set to work on recount standards. The contest case began with Sauls and was an appeal from him, so one would expect it to go back to him. But after the state supreme court reversed him, he recused, or removed, himself from the case. Later, Sauls revealed his decision was because he felt the action of the Florida Supreme Court was unconstitutional. In the hours after the state supreme court's ruling, Lewis gathered party representatives together in Tallahassee to set forth details. Lewis ordered any questionable Leon County ballots that had not already been trucked to Tallahassee to be shipped and ready for volunteers from both parties to start examining at the public library on Saturday at 8:00 a.m. He asked canvassing boards from the other counties to submit procedural plans to him by noon Saturday. If all went relatively smoothly, he figured workers would finish evaluating all 60,000 ballots by Sunday afternoon, less than two days.

> " Counting every legally cast vote cannot constitute irreparable harm. Preventing the recount from being completed will inevitably cast a cloud on the legitimacy of the election. . . . The Florida court's ruling reflects the basic principle, inherent in our Constitution and our democracy, that every legal vote should be counted. Accordingly, I dissent." [17]
> —JUSTICE STEVENS, US SUPREME COURT, DECEMBER 10, 2000, IN RESPONSE TO THE 5–4 DECISION TO HALT THE RECOUNT

But Lewis's plan was just that: a plan. In reality, the boards did not finish by Sunday afternoon. They had barely started counting on Saturday, December 9, when the US Supreme Court voted 5–4 to halt the manual counting and issued a **stay** to the recount.

In addition, the court treated its stay motion as a petition for a writ of certiorari and agreed to hear the *Bush v. Gore* case. Both sides had to file briefs by 4:00 p.m. on Sunday, December 10, in preparation for the justices to hear arguments in the case on Monday, December 11. It seemed the US Supreme Court would be the final authority in the controversial election after all, and none too soon. Electors were going to meet on December 18, but before that was the safe harbor date; if the issue in Florida was resolved by December 12, certification of the votes could not be challenged. Time was now a great pressure. ~

> "The counting of votes that are of questionable legality does in my view threaten irreparable harm to [Bush], and to the country, by casting a cloud upon what he claims to be the legitimacy of his election. Count first, and rule upon legality afterwards, is not a recipe for producing election results that have the public acceptance democratic stability requires."[18]
>
> —*JUSTICE SCALIA, RESPONDING TO JUSTICE STEVENS'S DISSENT IN THE DECISION TO STAY THE RECOUNT*

stay—A court-ordered stop.

Chapter 9

Bush v. Gore

*P*rior to taking their places on the bench on December 11, 2000, to hear arguments in *Bush v. Gore*, the US Supreme Court justices carefully read the briefs submitted by each side, as they do before every argument. On this thirty-third day of the election battle, the arguments must have come as no surprise to the justices. Bush claimed the Florida recount was unconstitutional; Gore claimed the recount was vital to upholding Americans' basic right to cast votes and have them counted.

Bush's Brief

For this case, Bush's team resurrected an argument in his brief the justices had refused to consider in *Bush v. Palm Beach County Canvassing Board*. They claimed the "plainly arbitrary, capricious, unequal, and standardless" Florida recount violated the equal protection clause of the Fourteenth Amendment to the US Constitution.[1]

Historically, the Fourteenth Amendment has been cited most frequently in cases of discrimination based on race, gender, and national origin. The Republicans argued that the Florida Supreme Court had bent the rules to favor Gore and penalize Bush. They believed the court had mandated an unjustifiable recount for which they neglected to set clear statewide standards. As a result, counties could conceivably evaluate a ballot

"EQUAL JUSTICE UNDER LAW"

Inscribed on the US Supreme Court Building, the phrase "Equal Justice Under Law" has been attributed to the building's architect, Cass Gilbert. He was apparently inspired by the words of a former chief justice, Melville Fuller:

> *By the Fourteenth Amendment the powers of the States in dealing with crime within their borders are not limited, but no State can deprive particular persons or classes of persons of equal and impartial justice under the law.*[2]

This phrase was too long to fit on the building, so Gilbert shortened it to its most basic message.

any way they wanted. An undervote accepted in one county might have been rejected in another county, and vice versa. Hence, voters—and Bush himself, his side believed—were being treated unequally.

Gore's Brief

The Gore team's brief suggested that not allowing a recount would do irreparable harm to the voters, not the candidates. The lawyers had written, "The only due process right even arguably implicated by this case is the

PREPARING FOR COURT

Before the US Supreme Court justices head to the bench, they stop in the robing room. There, each justice dons a plain black robe. Next, the justices perform a ritual that may seem unimportant but is actually steeped with significance: they shake hands. Justice Ginsburg explained, "It's a symbol of the work that we do as a collegial body."[3] It reminds them that, whatever their differences of opinion, they do their job together. A contentious case may divide them, but the handshake, in Justice O'Connor's opinion, helps prevent rifts from becoming longstanding: "If you take someone's hand and shake it, you're much less likely, I think, to hold a grudge. There's something about human contact that matters."[4] Soon after this gesture of civility, they line up in order of seniority and proceed into the courtroom, with the chief justice entering first.

right of voters to have their ballots counted."[5] The brief also addressed Bush's charge that the Florida court had violated Article II of the US Constitution by thwarting the power of the state legislature to choose electors and instead giving that power to itself. They argued instead that the Florida Supreme Court justices had only been following the system already established by the legislature.

In addition, as they had tried to prove in *Bush v. Palm Beach County Canvassing Board*, Gore and his team believed the Florida Supreme Court was simply doing its job, which was to interpret existing law. It had not created law.

The Arguments

At 11:00 a.m., the nine justices of the US Supreme Court stepped through the crimson drapes at the back of the courtroom and took their places on the bench. The giddy excitement that buzzed through the crowd in the first case ten days earlier was gone. The spectators had turned somber. The drama would finally, it seemed, come to an end.

Ted Olson took the lead for Bush, while David Boies represented Gore and Joseph Klock, a Miami lawyer, represented Harris. The secretary of state and the election commission had been named as **respondents** in the case, though Harris was essentially on the same side as the **petitioner**—her certification was being contested. The lawyers approached their oral arguments with a general knowledge of how the justices already viewed the case. Boies knew he did not have much chance of persuading staunch conservatives Rehnquist, Scalia, and Thomas to come over to his side. Scalia, especially, had not kept his disdain for the Florida justices' actions a secret. Olson and Klock figured they would have an uphill battle trying to convince traditionally liberal justices Stevens, Souter, Ginsburg, and Breyer there was a constitutional issue that necessitated their wresting control from the Florida courts. O'Connor and Kennedy had, in the past, sometimes sided with liberals, sometimes with conservatives, so they were the least predictable.

Almost as soon as Olson started his opening argument, Kennedy asked, "Can you begin by telling us our federal jurisdiction? Where's the federal question here?"[6] Olson noted Article II and its stipulation that state legislatures, not state courts, have authority in presidential elections. Kennedy seemed troubled by this argument. He indicated it set a dangerous precedent to assume a state legislature could not be held in check by its court system and its constitution. Such an assumption grants a state legislature a troubling amount of power.

While Kennedy's initial comments gave the Gore team a boost, the justice soon indicated to Olson that another of Bush's arguments might prove convincing. "I thought that your point was that the process is being conducted in violation of the Equal Protection Clause and it's standardless."[7] The Republicans saw an opening.

Throughout the oral arguments each justice chimed in with comments that indicated his or her concerns, except for Thomas, who had a policy of listening silently during hearings. Breyer and Souter each wondered aloud why the Florida court could not just draft a set of standards now and let the recount begin again. O'Connor seemed miffed that the Florida Supreme Court justices did not respond to the US Supreme Court's order for clarification on the previous case just days earlier, on December 4. O'Connor seemed

petitioner—The person or group who files a petition.
respondent—The person or group against whom a petition is filed.

exasperated by voters who did not follow the rules on Election Day, exclaiming at one point,

> *Well, why isn't the standard the one the voters are instructed to follow, for goodness sakes? I mean, it couldn't be clearer. I mean, why don't we go to that standard?*[8]

If O'Connor was less than likely to look with sympathy upon dimpled ballots, Ginsburg reminded Olson that the words "intent of the voter" come from Florida election code, straight from the legislators themselves.[9] Stevens agreed with Kennedy's assessment of the dangers of rampant legislative power.

> " The voters are instructed to detach the chads entirely, and the machine, as predicted, does not count those chads, where those instructions are not followed, there isn't any wrong."[11]
>
> —*JUSTICE SCALIA DURING ORAL ARGUMENTS IN* BUSH V. GORE

A bit of comic relief entered the charged atmosphere when Harris's lawyer, Joseph Klock, called justices by the wrong names during his turn to speak. Attempting to answer a question from Justice Stevens, Klock began, "Well, Justice Brennan. . . ."[10] Brennan had retired from the court in 1990 and had died in 1997. A flustered

Klock apologized. He fumbled again, referring to Justice Souter as Justice Breyer. "I'm Justice Souter, you've got to cut that out," the justice admonished, and friendly laughs filled the courtroom when Klock jokingly responded, "I will now give up."[12] Justice Scalia, known for his sly sense of humor, immediately called from the bench, "Mr. Klock? I'm Scalia!"[13]

Finally, it was Boies's turn to speak. Rehnquist attempted to get the facts straight, asking about the number of ballots that needed to be recounted. Boies explained the figure of 177,000 that Rehnquist questioned included overvotes and the number of undervotes to examine was approximately 60,000.[14]

The arguments quickly came to an end. Once again, it was time to wait. The justices needed to deliberate.

The Justices Decide

As the justices entered the conference room to deliberate, they had much to consider. They had the words of Olson, who addressed, among other things, Boies's assertion that the standard for counting votes in Florida was "whether or not the intent of the voter is reflected by the ballot."[15] Olson had told the court,

We have standards that are different throughout 64 different counties; we've got only undercounts being considered, where an indentation on a ballot will now be counted as a vote, but other ballots that may have indentations aren't going to be counted at all.[16]

It was not fair to his client, Olson suggested, or to the American people.

Unlike many US Supreme Court cases, which are not decided for weeks or months, *Bush v. Gore* was decided quickly. On the evening of December 12, the ruling was revealed. In a close 5–4 vote, the ruling supported Olson, though the dissension within the court's ranks was obvious as soon as the justices exited the conference room. Normally, the justices reassemble at the bench to issue an opinion, and the justice who authored it summarizes the majority ruling aloud. But following the ruling, the nine judges simply left, while copies of their per curiam decision circulated in the press room.

Kennedy, with O'Connor working closely with him, drafted the **majority opinion**. It reaffirmed Bush's interpretation of the equal protection issue: "Having once granted the right to vote on equal terms, the State

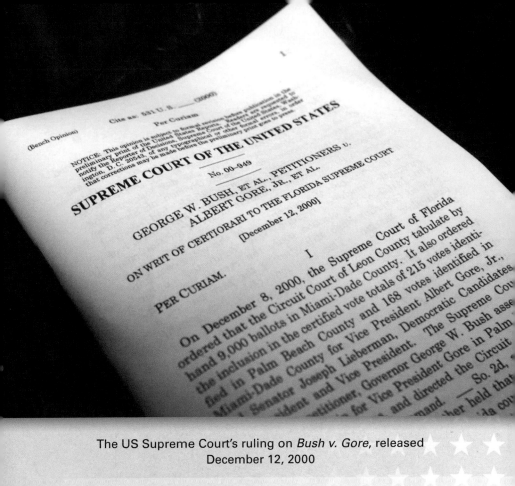

The US Supreme Court's ruling on *Bush v. Gore*, released
December 12, 2000

may not, by later arbitrary and disparate treatment, value
one person's vote over that of another."[17] The undervote
recounts authorized by the Florida Supreme Court was
an example of such disparate treatment. Essentially,
the issue was that the recount ruling by the Florida

majority opinion—An explanation of the reasoning behind the
majority decision of the Supreme Court.

Supreme Court granted some votes greater protection than others, and this action violated the equal protection clause of the Fourteenth Amendment. While honoring the intent of the voter was an admirable goal in theory, Kennedy and the others in the majority did not see it working under these circumstances. They lambasted the Florida court:

> The question before the Court is not whether local entities, in the exercise of their expertise, may develop different systems for implementing elections. Instead, we are presented with a situation where a state court with the power to assure uniformity has ordered a statewide recount with minimal procedural safeguards. When a court orders a statewide remedy, there must be at least some assurance that the rudimentary requirements of equal treatment and fundamental fairness are satisfied.[18]

The ruling went on to address the impossibility of completing a recount in a manner that agrees with the US Constitution:

> *It is obvious that the recount cannot be conducted in compliance with the requirements of equal protection and due process without substantial additional work. It would require not only the adoption (after opportunity for argument) of adequate statewide standards for determining what is a legal vote, and practicable procedures to implement them, but also orderly **judicial review** of any disputed matters that might arise.*[20]

In other words, fixing the situation would take time and effort. Rules would need to be created, processes for following the rules would need to be established, and, if necessary, courts would need to be involved to settle any issues that would come up. Simply put, the ruling noted,

> *Because it is evident that any recount seeking to meet the December 12 date will be unconstitutional for the reasons we have discussed, we reverse the*

judicial review—The power of a court to examine an executive or legislative act and to deny the act effect if it is unconstitutional.

judgment of the Supreme Court of Florida ordering a recount to proceed.[21]

Rehnquist, Scalia, and Thomas—the three most conservative justices—issued a statement separate from the majority opinion to explain why they also thought Bush was correct in citing Article II violations. The three noted they usually left it to state courts to deal with issues of state law, but this case presented a unique situation. The three justices decided the Florida court had created new law, or at least "impermissibly distorted" existing election laws "beyond what a fair reading required, in violation of Article II."[22]

The Dissents

In their dissents to the majority, Breyer and Souter agreed with the majority that lack of a uniform standard made the recount unacceptably arbitrary, but they felt there was a viable solution: have the Florida Supreme Court set one. The majority ruling did not leave an opening for this possibility:

> " The Court was wrong to take this case. It was wrong to grant a stay. It should now vacate that stay and permit the Florida Supreme Court to decide whether the recount should resume."[23]
>
> —*JUSTICE BREYER, IN HIS DISSENT,* BUSH V. GORE, *DECEMBER 12, 2000*

Under due consideration of the difficulties identified to this point, it is obvious that the recount cannot be conducted in compliance with the requirements of equal protection and due process without substantial additional work.[24]

December 12, the safe harbor deadline for states to appoint their electors—members to the Electoral College—without risk of having them challenged by Congress, had reached an end. There was no time for additional work: case closed.

Breyer and Souter had a different deadline in mind: December 18, the date set for the Electoral College to vote. Florida would forfeit safe harbor protection by not having electors in place by the twelfth, but the state would gain six extra days for counting. Souter, in his own dissenting opinion—signed by Stevens, Ginsburg, and Breyer—saw no reason for his colleagues to assume the process could not be completed by then. Souter's solution was to "remand the case to the courts of Florida with instructions to establish uniform standards for evaluating the several types of ballots that have prompted differing treatments."[25] In other words, he wanted the case returned to Florida for the state to create a statewide method for assessing ballots.

SAFE HARBOR

In general, a safe harbor is a provision of a law or rule that lays out reasonably clear-cut rules that, when followed, will make a party safe, or okay. With regard to the recount, Title 3, Chapter 1, Section 5 of the federal statute explains that if a state resolved all contests to the choice of electors at least six days before the date prescribed for voting—in this case, December 12—the certification is binding, in the sense that when the electoral votes are opened before Congress, a challenge to those electors would not be considered in Congress.

The Florida Supreme Court had previously indicated a desire to take advantage of the safe harbor provision by wrapping up everything by December 12, the safe harbor deadline, because that was the desire of the state legislature. The US Supreme Court ruled, in effect, that the state's supreme court wanted to take advantage of the safe harbor, but because there was no way of doing so while holding a recount that met constitutional standards, there could be no recount. The Florida court had indicated it wanted both a recount and the safe harbor, but it had not indicated which it would choose if it could have only one.

In her own dissent, Ginsburg, with Stevens's agreement, mentioned an even later deadline: December 27. It was "the date on which Congress, if it has not received a State's electoral votes, shall request the state secretary of state to send certified results immediately."[26] In addition, Ginsburg noted disagreement on a constitutional claim by the majority, writing,

> *I agree with Justice Stevens that petitioners have not presented a substantial equal protection claim. Ideally, perfection would be the appropriate standard for judging the recount. But we live in an imperfect world, one in which thousands of votes have not been counted. I cannot agree that the recount adopted by the Florida court, flawed as it may be, would yield a result any less fair or precise than the certification that preceded that recount.[27]*

It was obvious from their four written dissents that Stevens, Souter, Ginsburg, and Breyer passionately disagreed with the majority on many levels. The most stirring comments came from Stevens. He ended his opinion by suggesting the majority's ruling in *Bush v. Gore* represented a "cynical" lack of confidence in the ability of the Florida courts to act impartially and administer justice.[28] He also implied that Americans' faith in their entire judicial system would take a blow. Boldly, he announced,

> *Although we may never know with complete certainty the identity of the winner of this year's Presidential election, the identity of the loser is*

The 2000 US presidential election dominated other nations'
newspapers. The US Supreme Court ruling in December made
headlines in Hong Kong.

perfectly clear. It is the Nation's confidence in the
judge as an impartial guardian of the rule of law.[29]

Stevens stopped just short of a direct accusation of partisanship, but, in the coming weeks, critics of the decision would more bluntly continue this line of thought. They would denounce the justices in the majority for butting in and handing the presidency to their own preferred candidate: Bush. ~

> "To recount these [60,000 undervotes] manually would be a tall order, but before this Court stayed the effort to do that the courts of Florida were ready to do their best to get that job done. There is no justification for denying the State the opportunity to try to count all disputed ballots now."[30]
>
> —*JUSTICE SOUTER, IN HIS DISSENT, BUSH V. GORE, DECEMBER 12, 2000*

Chapter 10

Justice Served or Election Stolen?

"Just moments ago, I spoke with George W. Bush, and congratulated him on becoming the forty-third president of the United States—and I promised him that I wouldn't call him back this time."[1] The candidate not known for his sense of humor could finally crack a joke. On the night of Wednesday, December 13, Gore had reached the end of a surreal 36 days in which it seemed a winner in the 2000 presidential election might never be chosen.

Flanked at the podium by his wife, Tipper, and their four children, Gore thanked the supporters assembled before him at the Old Executive Office Building, next door to the White House. In his televised eight-minute speech, he urged against bitterness toward the US Supreme Court:

> While I strongly disagree with the court's decision, I accept it. I accept the finality of the outcome, which will be ratified next Monday in the Electoral College. And tonight for the sake of our unity as a people and the strength of our democracy, I offer my concession.[2]

Legally, Gore had to concede. After the US Supreme Court's ruling, he and his attorneys considered filing a brief with the Florida Supreme Court asking for all indented undervote ballots to be counted. But the December 12 safe harbor deadline, which the majority ruling treated as decisive—Florida could not have a recount by the date, so no recount—made this endeavor hopeless. After 24 years in Washington DC serving his country as a congressman, a senator, and vice president, Gore planned to go home to Tennessee

FINAL CERTIFICATION

After the US Supreme Court's ruling, Florida's general election returns were certified. The final tally was 2,912,790 for Bush and 2,912,253 for Gore. Each man had won 49 percent of the votes. Bush won the state by 537 votes.[3]

Bush flashed a "W" sign, his middle initial and a nickname, December 13, 2000, after addressing the nation following the US Supreme Court's landmark decision.

and, as he said in his speech, "mend some fences, literally and figuratively."[4] He would try to put partisan animosity behind him.

Responses to the Ruling

Unlike Gore, other Democrats openly expressed bitterness. Angry letters poured in to the US Supreme Court, some accompanied by voter registration cards. If our votes are not counted, then take these, they are useless, the surrendered cards implied. Celebrity lawyer and renowned liberal Vincent Bugliosi wrote a scathing article in the *Nation* that went so far as to call the majority justices' behavior treasonous. He said the five judges deliberately shunned the will of voters, bending and stretching the law whichever way they could to get Bush into office:

> And if the Court's five-member majority was concerned not about Bush but the voters themselves, as they fervently claimed to be, then under what conceivable theory would they, in effect, tell these voters, "We're so concerned that some of you undervoters may lose your vote under the different Florida county standards that we're going to solve

BUSH THE VICTOR

After Gore conceded, Bush gave his victory speech from the Texas House of Representatives in Austin. In it, he echoed Gore's call for reconciliation:

> I was not elected to serve one party, but to serve one nation. Whether you voted for me or not, I will do my best to serve your interests, and I will work to earn your respect.[5]

He made little reference to the postelection craziness except to say, "I am thankful for America, and thankful that we are able to resolve our electoral differences in a peaceful way."[6]

the problem by making sure that none of you undervoters have your votes counted?"[7]

He believed only voters, not candidates, had grounds for seeking shelter under the Fourteenth Amendment's equal protection clause: "What happened here is that Bush leaped in and tried to profit from a hypothetical wrong inflicted on someone else."[8] Saying Bugliosi was angry would be an understatement.

Other commentators sounded Bugliosi's charge of judicial activism. They felt the US Supreme Court butted in when it should have stayed away. Larry D. Kramer, a law professor at Stanford University, contributed an opinion piece to the *New York Times* in which he compared the Rehnquist court's decisions with those of past courts and found the Rehnquist court was

JUDICIAL ACTIVISM

When judges use their power in the courts to promote a specific political or social agenda, they are said to be practicing judicial activism. Critics of the court who charge it with judicial activism often use the argument that activist judges are trying to make new laws and are not just interpreting existing laws. It is common for the losers of a case to accuse the court of activism as a way of expressing their disagreement with the decision.

less "[respectful] to other branches of government" and had "abandoned restraint."[9] He concluded that, though conservative judicial philosophy usually leans toward honoring states' rights, "The Florida case shows that state governments get no more deference than other branches of government."[10] He predicted the one good to come out of *Bush v. Gore* would be a Supreme Court humbled by backlash—a court less convinced of "its own supremacy."[11]

Not every pundit hurled criticism. Some praised the Supreme Court for getting involved in what, according to supporters, was obviously a constitutional issue, though the justices knew it would open them up to allegations of partisanship. Nelson Lund, a professor of constitutional law at George Mason University, offered a detailed response to the case. In "The Unbearable Rightness of *Bush v. Gore*," he listed "supposed sins" of the majority opinion in the case that had been named by critics of the court and its ruling:

> *The Court should have refused to hear the case for fear of creating an "appearance" of political partiality. The Court should have refused to apply its Fourteenth Amendment precedents for fear of having them taken seriously in future cases.*

The Court should have ignored the Florida court's one-day-old decision about the meaning of Florida law, thereby inviting that court to commit further violations of federal law. The Court should have refused to apply well-established federal law in this case because of a supposed commitment by the Court's conservatives to some notion of federalism [credited] to them by people who have apparently never read their opinions.[12]

Lund's response to these opinions was succinct and clear: "None of these criticisms has the slightest merit."[13] He expanded on this idea in his conclusion:

Faced with a gross violation of law by a subordinate court, the Bush v. Gore *majority did exactly what an **appellate court** is supposed to do. It reversed the erroneous decision and upheld the law.*[14]

The justices themselves rarely spoke about the case publicly. When they did, only the naturally argumentative Scalia seemed to enjoy firing back at critics. When interviewed about the case in later years, O'Connor often brought up the unofficial recounts

appellate court—A court that can review and reverse the judgment of a lower court.

newspapers such as the *Miami Herald* conducted after the election's final certification to show the decision really did not change anything—Bush would have won anyway. Souter, however, was reported to have been so devastated by the Supreme Court's role in the election that he considered resigning. An introverted bachelor who rarely mingled in Washington's social circles, he defined himself by his work. He took his vow to be an impartial arbiter, or judge, of the law to heart, and the thought that some of his colleagues had let partisanship color their judgment affected him deeply. In the end, Souter stayed.

The nature of the US Supreme Court is such that the justices can never escape dissension and difficult issues. But, as Ginsburg has explained, dwelling on grievances can prevent a judge from effectively doing the job he or she was appointed to do. Ginsburg's philosophy is to concentrate on the present and future instead of the past:

> *You do your best in every case. But when it's over, it's over, and you don't look back. You just go on to the next case and give it your all.*[15]

Florida after the Ruling

The state of Florida would take time to get back to normal after the 2000 election, especially Palm Beach County. *Palm Beach Post* reporter Frank Cerabino noted that, in a little over a month, Palm Beach had gone from being known for its golf resorts, sunshine, and the occasional hurricane to being "the baffling center of a baffling state."[16] Instead of images of retirees playing golf, the place now conjured visions of confused elderly voters punching the wrong hole, too many holes, or no hole at all in their ballots. Some residents were able to maintain a sense of humor about what happened. Butterfly ballot–shaped jewelry and menus began popping up at local businesses.

This was not the case for everyone. For LePore, who had adopted the much maligned ballot for

> "This peaceful transfer of authority is rare in history, yet common in our country. With a simple oath, we affirm old traditions, and make new beginnings. As I begin, I thank President Clinton for his service to our nation. And I thank Vice President Gore for a contest conducted with spirit, and ended with grace."[17]
>
> —GEORGE W. BUSH, INAUGURAL ADDRESS, JANUARY 20, 2001

her county, the situation had caused great pain and frustration. Democrats blamed her for Gore's defeat. LePore explained,

> *People in my own party [were] making all these accusations [saying that] I was paid off by the Republicans and just all this garbage, a petition going around calling for my resignation.*[18]

Still, LePore hoped things would improve for her and for Florida. She told an interviewer,

> *I think it's a good learning experience. They say of all bad things, something good comes. [We've got new] technology . . . and public awareness, voters hopefully understanding that their votes will count.*[19]

But LePore was perhaps more hopeful than others. For Americans to regain confidence in the voting process, certain things would have to change. ∽

Chapter 11

The Legacy of
Bush v. Gore

*T*he events of November and December 2000
that led to *Bush v. Gore*, of course, influenced
the United States by determining the winner of the
election. In addition, they ultimately affected voting
in Florida and election-centered lawsuits.

Florida's New Voting Law

Bush's swearing in as president in January 2001 did
not end the voting issue in Florida. The debacle that
was the 2000 presidential election led to the Florida
State Legislature passing the Electoral Reform Act
of 2001.

Governor Jeb Bush signed new election reform legislation on May 9, 2001, that resulted from the 2000 presidential election debacle in his state.

Keeping in mind the myriad issues the 2000 presidential election brought to light in Florida's voting process, the state's 2001 legislation set in motion many improvements. Punch-card voting systems were abolished and funds were allocated for new equipment.

Also, proof of voter eligibility was relaxed. For example, a citizen whose name does not appear on his or her precinct's roster can cast a vote and verify eligibility later. And standards for statewide recounts were established.

An Increase in Lawsuits

As for the nation as a whole, *Bush v. Gore* and the rest of the postelection drama led many more Americans to court. A 2009 study conducted by election law expert Richard L. Hasen found that the number of election-related lawsuits in the United States more than doubled after 2000. Before that landmark year in politics, the average number of cases per year stood at 94. Afterward, the average rose to 237, reaching a high of 361 during the next big election year: 2004.[1]

Writing in the online magazine *Slate* in 2010 to mark the ten-year anniversary of *Bush v. Gore*, Hasen attributed the increase to changed attitudes about the US electoral process:

> Bush v. Gore *taught political operatives and everyone else that there are significant problems in how we administer our elections and that when contests are close enough to be within the margin of litigation, it makes sense to fight on rather than concede.*[3]

Now that Americans had seen and learned how the system worked—or did not work—they could no longer accept the official results of a tight race without a legal fight.

Subsequent lawsuits have addressed inequalities the Florida ordeal highlighted, including disparities in voting equipment and voter education throughout the country. In *Southwest Voter Registration Education Project v. Shelley*, the plaintiff filed suit in California in 2003 to fight for a mandate like the one passed in Florida, which would update the state's voting machines. Plaintiffs argued that punch-card systems, with their dimpled chads and other disasters, violated voters' equal protection rights. A three-judge panel of the circuit court ruled in favor of the plaintiff, but that decision was later vacated by a larger panel of the same court in an **en banc decision**.

Infamous Phrase

In 2006, lawyers in Ohio working on a similar voting rights case, *League of Women Voters of Ohio v. Blackwell*, cited *Bush v. Gore*, but to no avail. A circuit court judge objected on the grounds that "we should heed the Supreme Court's own warning and limit the reach

THE ELECTORAL COLLEGE DEBATE

Arguments for and against the Electoral College have existed since its inception, and they intensified in the wake of the 2000 election. Those who oppose it think the president should be elected by popular vote and argue that winning the most popular votes and losing the election is unfair. This has been the case for four presidential candidates: Andrew Jackson in 1824, Samuel Tilden in 1876, Grover Cleveland in 1888, and Al Gore in 2000. Such critics also believe scrapping the current system would encourage voter participation and the entrance of minority parties in presidential races. Those who want to keep the current system argue that it has served the country well for more than 200 years, so the nation might as well keep it. Some also argue that it forces candidates to focus more on small states, as well as large ones, because they have a disproportionately high number of electors.

of *Bush v. Gore* to the peculiar and extraordinary facts of that case."[4] The judge was referring to what has become an infamous phrase in the Supreme Court's majority opinion: "Our consideration is limited to the present circumstances, for the problem of equal protection in election processes generally presents many complexities."[5] In their ruling, the justices discouraged future courts from applying their findings elsewhere.

In an opinion piece in the *New Yorker*, author Jeffrey Toobin noted judges' adherence to this decree when reflecting on the case upon its tenth anniversary. He noted how *Roe v. Wade*, the 1973 landmark decision that legalized abortion, was cited in US Supreme Court rulings more than 65 times in the ten years following the decision. In contrast, the justices had not cited *Bush v. Gore* a single time. Toobin wrote,

> *Both sides had their reasons for [giving] the decision to history and leaving it there. . . . Even at the time,* Bush v. Gore *was treated as a kind of novelty item, a one-off decision that applied only to the*

---

en banc decision—A decision by the full court, generally all the judges appointed to a given district or circuit.

peculiar facts then before the Justices. The majority itself seemed to want it that way.[6]

Toobin went on to address judicial activism, saying the justices appeared to let politics play a greater role in decisions than they had previously and have done so even more since. Ultimately, Toobin believed the case disgraced the court:

> *Many of the issues before the Supreme Court combine law and politics in ways that are impossible to separate. It is, moreover, unreasonable to expect the Justices to operate in a world [completely] cut off from the gritty motives of Democrats and Republicans. But the least we can expect from these men and women is that at politically charged moments—indeed, especially at those times—they apply the same principles that guide them in everyday cases. This, ultimately, is the tragedy of* Bush v. Gore. *The case didn't just scar the Court's record; it damaged the Court's honor.*[7]

Richard L. Hasen, a professor of law and political science at the University of California–Irvine, presented a different view on the legacy of *Bush v. Gore*. In 2010, he wrote,

GORE AND BUSH AFTER THE RULING

After the 2000 election and ruling, Gore left politics for environmental activism. He wrote an acclaimed book about climate change, *An Inconvenient Truth*, and starred in the companion Academy Award–winning documentary film. He—along with the United Nations Intergovernmental Panel on Climate Change—was awarded the 2007 Nobel Peace Prize for his efforts to increase awareness about the threat of global warming.

Bush went on to steer the nation through the tragedy of the terrorist attacks on September 11, 2001, and into the controversial Iraq War. In 2004, Bush beat Democrat John Kerry to win a second term. His victory included winning Florida. There, he beat Kerry by an undisputed margin of 380,978 votes.[9]

The real lesson of the Florida fiasco (not merely Bush v. Gore) is about something else: the undermining of the public's faith in the fairness of American elections. This has triggered an ongoing war over their administration.[8]

Clearly, critics have not felt the US Supreme Court acted as it did for the right reasons. However, there is potential good that could come from the court's landmark decision and has come from what happened in Florida. It would be difficult to disagree that the

In 2007, Nobel Prize recipient Gore visited President Bush at the White House. The decision in *Bush v. Gore* had changed their lives and history.

best guarantee of accurate election results is an equitable voting system. And it would be hard to deny that rich or poor, man or woman, old or young, every eligible voter has the right to have his or her vote count. ~

TIMELINE OF EVENTS
AND RULINGS

November 7   Americans vote for a new president.

November 8   State code triggers a mandatory machine recount of all votes in Florida.

November 9   The Florida Democratic Executive Committee requests manual recounts in Palm Beach, Volusia, Broward, and Miami-Dade Counties.

November 11   George H. W. Bush files suit to block the manual recounts.

November 13   The federal district court denies Bush's request.

November 14   Volusia completes its manual recount.

November 15   Secretary of State Katherine Harris rejects arguments for a deadline extension from Palm Beach, Broward, and Miami-Dade and refuses to accept their manual recount totals.

November 20   *Palm Beach County Canvassing Board v. Harris* is argued before the Florida Supreme Court regarding Harris including manual recount returns.

November 21   The Florida Supreme Court allows manual recounts to continue and sets a new deadline for the four counties to submit their results.

November 22   Bush appeals the Florida Supreme Court's decision to the US Supreme Court.

November 26   Harris certifies Bush the winner in Florida.

November 27	Al Gore files suit in Leon County Circuit Court to contest election results in three counties.
December 1	The US Supreme Court hears arguments in *Bush v. Palm Beach County Canvassing Board*, which fought the recount deadline extension.
December 4	The US Supreme Court sends *Bush v. Palm Beach County Canvassing Board* back to the Florida Supreme Court; Judge N. Sanders Sauls rejects Gore's contest of the election.
December 7	The Florida Supreme Court hears arguments in Gore's appeal of Sauls's ruling.
December 8	The Florida Supreme Court orders an immediate manual recount of all of Florida's undervotes.
December 9	Florida's statewide manual recount begins. Later in the day, the US Supreme Court halts the recount.
December 10	Attorneys for both sides file briefs for the US Supreme Court case *Bush v. Gore*.
December 11	The US Supreme Court hears oral arguments in *Bush v. Gore*.
December 12	The US Supreme Court halts the manual recounts, deciding who will become president: Bush.
December 13	Gore concedes the election.
December 18	Members of the Electoral College vote: Gore receives 266 votes and Bush receives 271, making him the forty-third president of the United States.

GLOSSARY

canvassing board
> A three-person team in each of Florida's counties responsible for supervising elections there.

certification
> The official confirmation of returns in an election.

constituency
> The people who live in an electoral district.

contest
> The legal method in Florida by which an unsuccessful candidate for public office can dispute the results of an election after they have been certified.

disenfranchise
> To deprive the right to vote.

elector
> Someone who can vote in an election; a member of the Electoral College.

intent of the voter
> The standard under Florida law by which a vote should be counted: if the county canvassing board can justifiably discern which candidate a voter intended to mark on the ballot, the vote should be counted.

lobbyist

> Someone who tries to persuade or influence people, especially public officials.

machine recount

> The process of running ballots through the tabulation machines again to check the totals in a close election.

manual recount

> The process of recounting votes by hand that have already been counted by machine.

partisan

> To follow, adhere to, or support a political party or group.

pundit

> A critic or person who gives opinions.

swing state

> During a presidential election, a state where polls show voters are undecided; candidates typically devote a great deal of their time and attention to swing states.

BRIEFS

Petitioner

George W. Bush, governor of Texas, Republican presidential candidate

Respondent

Albert Gore Jr., vice president of the United States, Democratic presidential candidate

Date of Ruling

December 12, 2000

Summary of Impacts

In November 2000, the US presidential election came down to the state of Florida. The candidates were separated by fewer than 2,000 votes—a difference that required an automatic recount per Florida's election law. When voting irregularities came to light, Gore and Democrats called for a manual recount in four counties. Undervotes and overvotes became issues as canvassing boards and volunteers began examining ballots that had been cast. Bush and Republicans called for a halt to recounting, noting how its inconsistent application violated voters' rights—all votes must be recounted using the same process, or no votes can be recounted. The recount led to 36 days of uncertainty that held the attention of the nation and the world while the winner of the state's popular vote remained in dispute. This fight for the nation's highest office led to numerous lawsuits by the candidates as well as by citizens.

Ultimately, the issue went to the US Supreme Court—twice—which finally ruled in a split decision in favor of Bush and his argument that stressed the lack of consistency in recounting. The case made history as different areas of the election process were highlighted while the battle for the presidency was fought in county, state, and federal courts. These included ballot design, voter education, tabulation machines, recount procedures, and the Electoral College. The US Supreme Court's decision was met with celebration by Bush supporters, who thought Bush was the rightful winner, and derision by Gore supporters, who thought the court had interjected politics into a close election of great importance to the nation.

Quote

"Although we may never know with complete certainty the identity of the winner of this year's Presidential election, the identity of the loser is perfectly clear. It is the Nation's confidence in the judge as an impartial guardian of the rule of law."

—Justice John Paul Stevens, in his dissent to the majority opinion of the US Supreme Court in Bush v. Gore, *decided on December 12, 2000*

ADDITIONAL RESOURCES

Selected Bibliography

Correspondents of the *New York Times*. *36 Days: The Complete Chronicle of the 2000 Presidential Election*. New York: Henry Holt, 2001. Print.

Dionne, E. J., Jr., and William Kristol, eds. *Bush v. Gore: The Court Cases and the Commentary*. Washington, DC: Brookings, 2001. Print.

Merzer, Martin, and the staff of the *Miami Herald*. *The Miami Herald Report: Democracy Held Hostage*. New York: St. Martin's, 2001. Print.

Toobin, Jeffrey. *The Nine: Inside the Secret World of the Supreme Court*. New York: Anchor, 2008. Print.

Toobin, Jeffrey. *Too Close to Call: The Thirty-Six-Day Battle to Decide the 2000 Election*. New York: Random, 2001. Print.

Further Readings

Hartman, Gary R., Roy M. Mersky, and Cindy L. Tate. *Landmark Supreme Court Cases: The Most Influential Decisions of the Supreme Court of the United States*. New York: Facts on File, 2004. Print.

Lamb, Brian, Susan Swain, and Mark Farkas, eds. *The Supreme Court: A C-SPAN Book Featuring the Justices in Their Own Words*. New York: PublicAffairs, 2010. Print.

Mieczkowski, Yanek. *The Routledge Historical Atlas of Presidential Elections*. New York: Routledge, 2001. Print.

Web Links

To learn more about *Bush v. Gore*, visit ABDO Publishing Company online at **www.abdopublishing.com**. Web sites about *Bush v. Gore* are featured on our Book Links page. These links are routinely monitored and updated to provide the most current information available.

Places to Visit

Florida Supreme Court
500 South Duval Street, Tallahassee, FL 32399-1927
850-488-0125
www.floridasupremecourt.org/education/index.shtml
The court offers tours and educational programs, including the programs Mock Oral Arguments and Making My Vote Count!

Smithsonian National Museum of American History
National Mall, Fourteenth Street and Constitution Avenue, Washington, DC 20560
202-633-1000
http://americanhistory.si.edu
Explore US history, including presidential history in the exhibit "The American Presidency: A Glorious Burden."

US Supreme Court
One First Street NE, Washington, DC 20543
202-479-3000
www.supremecourt.gov/visiting/visiting.aspx
Visitors are encouraged to explore the building. Educational programs include lectures, exhibits, and a film specifically for visitors.

SOURCE NOTES

Chapter 1. Not Over Yet

1. Federal Election Commission. "Distribution of Electoral Votes." *FEC.gov*. Federal Election Commission, 3 Oct. 2003. Web. 8 May 2012.

2. "2000 Presidential Election Electoral Vote Data." *USElectionAtlas. org*. David Leip, 2012. Web. 10 May 2012.

3. Jeffrey Toobin. *Too Close to Call: The Thirty-Six-Day Battle to Decide the 2000 Election*. New York: Random, 2001. Print. 25.

4. Ibid.

5. David Bauder. "Networks Try to Explain Blown Call." *Washingtonpost.com*. Associated Press, 2000. Web. 8 May 2012.

Chapter 2. A Tight Race

1. "Top 10 Bushisms." *Time.com*. Time, 2012. Web. 8 May 2012.

2. Jacob Weisberg. "W.'s Greatest Hits." *Slate*. Slate Group, 12 Jan. 2009. Web. 8 May 2012.

3. Ibid.

4. Ibid.

5. David Barstow and Don Van Natta Jr. "Examining the Vote; How Bush Took Florida: Mining the Absentee Vote." *New York Times*. New York Times, 15 July 2001. Web. 8 May 2012.

Chapter 3. Ballot Issues

1. Julian M. Pleasants. *Hanging Chads: The Inside Story of the 2000 Presidential Recount in Florida*. New York: Palgrave Macmillan, 2004. Print. 78.

2. Ibid. 79.

3. US Census Bureau. "Palm Beach County, Florida." *Census.gov*. US Census Bureau, 31 Jan. 2012. Web. 8 May 2012.

4. Christine Stapleton and George Bennett. "New Census Numbers Show Palm Beach County's 85-Plus Crowd Grows 41%." *Palm Beach Post News*. Palm Beach Post, 5 May 2011. Web. 8 May 2012.

5. NIA Press Office and Census Bureau. "Dramatic Changes in U.S. Aging Highlighted in New Census, NIH Report." *National Institute on Aging*. National Institutes of Health, 27 Sept. 2011. Web. 8 May 2012.

6. Julian M. Pleasants. *Hanging Chads: The Inside Story of the 2000 Presidential Recount in Florida*. New York: Palgrave Macmillan, 2004. Print. 78.

7. Don Van Natta Jr. and Dana Canedy. "The 2000 Elections: The Palm Beach Ballot; Florida Democrats Say Ballot's Design Hurt Gore." *New York Times*. New York Times, 9 Nov. 2000. Web. 8 May 2012.

8. Richard L. Smith. "A Statistical Assessment of Buchanan's Vote in Palm Beach County." *University of North Carolina Web site*. n.p., 18 Nov. 2000. Web. 8 May 2012.

9. Howard Gillman. *The Votes that Counted: How the Court Decided the 2000 Presidential Election*. Chicago: U of Chicago P, 2001. 23. *Google Book Search*. Web. 10 May 2012.

10. Dennis Cauchon and Jim Drinkard. "Florida Voter Errors Cost Gore the Election." *USA Today*. USA Today, 11 May 2001. Web. 8 May 2012.

11. Bob Drogin and Richard O'Reilly. "Many Voters Simply Did It Wrong." *Los Angeles Times*. Los Angeles Times, 12 Nov. 2001. Web. 8 May 2012.

12. David Gonzalez. "Counting the Vote: The Race Factor; Blacks, Citing Flaws, Seek Inquiry into Florida Vote." *New York Times*. New York Times, 11 Nov. 2000. Web. 8 May 2012.

13. Julian M. Pleasants. *Hanging Chads: The Inside Story of the 2000 Presidential Recount in Florida*. New York: Palgrave Macmillan, 2004. Print. 64.

14. Nada Mourtada-Sabbah and Bruce E. Cain, eds. *The Political Question Doctrine and the Supreme Court of the United States*. Lanham, MD: Lexington, 2007. 205. *Google Book Search*. Web. 10 May 2012.

Chapter 4. The Protest

1. Jeffrey Toobin. *Too Close to Call: The Thirty-Six-Day Battle to Decide the 2000 Election*. New York: Random House, 2001. Print. 71.

2. Ibid. 69.

3. Julian M. Pleasants. *Hanging Chads: The Inside Story of the 2000 Presidential Recount in Florida*. New York: Palgrave Macmillan, 2004. Print. 66.

4. Kristi Reid Bronson. "Deadline for Certification on County Results." *Division of Elections*. State of Florida, 13 Nov. 2000. Web. 8 May 2012.

5. "Florida Election Deadline." *FraudFactor*. FraudFactor.com, 5 Jan. 2001. Web. 8 May 2012.

6. Associated Press and Reuters. "Election Heads to Court." *ABC News*. ABC News Internet Ventures, Yahoo! - ABC News Network, 2012. Web. 8 May 2012.

7. Ibid.

8. Jeffrey Toobin. *Too Close to Call: The Thirty-Six-Day Battle to Decide the 2000 Election*. New York: Random, 2001. Print. 100–101.

9. "14th Amendment." *Legal Information Institute*. Cornell University Law School, n.d. Web. 8 May 2012.

10. Ibid.

11. Vincent Bugliosi. *The Betrayal of America: How the Supreme Court Undermined the Constitution and Chose Our President*. New York: Thunder's Mouth/Nation, 2001. Print. 121.

12. Jeffrey Toobin. *Too Close to Call: The Thirty-Six-Day Battle to Decide the 2000 Election*. New York: Random, 2001. Print. 115.

13. "Officials in Palm Beach Submit Results." *New York Times*. New York Times, 14 Nov. 2000. Web. 8 May 2012.

Chapter 5. Stopping Harris

1. Kristi Reid Bronson. "Text of Katherine Harris Legal Opinion." *ABC News*. ABC News Internet Ventures, Yahoo! - ABC News Network, 2012. Web. 8 May 2012.

2. Richard L. Berke and Janet Elder. "Counting the Vote: The Poll; Americans Patiently Awaiting Election Outcome." *New York Times*. New York Times, 14 Nov. 2000. Web. 8 May 2012.

3. E. J. Dionne Jr. and William Kristol, eds. Bush v. Gore: *The Court Cases and the Commentary*. Washington, DC: Brookings, 2001. Print. 22.

4. Julian M. Pleasants. *Hanging Chads: The Inside Story of the 2000 Presidential Recount in Florida*. New York: Palgrave Macmillan, 2004. Print. 66.

5. Jeffrey Toobin. *Too Close to Call: The Thirty-Six-Day Battle to Decide the 2000 Election*. New York: Random, 2001. Print. 72.

6. Dexter Filkins. "The 2000 Election: Palm Beach; At the Epicenter of a Voting Dispute, a Chasm in the Streets." *New York Times*. New York Times, 10 Nov. 2000. Web. 8 May 2000.

7. Julian M. Pleasants. *Hanging Chads: The Inside Story of the 2000 Presidential Recount in Florida*. New York: Palgrave Macmillan, 2004. Print. 81.

8. Rob Longley. "County's Embattled Election Supervisor Will Not Quit." *Boca Raton News* 22 Dec. 2000. 5A. *Google Book Search*. Web. 10 May 2012.

9. Richard L. Berke, "Counting the Vote: The Overview; Republican Rejects Offer that 2 Sides Accept a County by Hand." *New York Times*. New York Times, 16 Nov. 2000. Web. 23 Mar. 2012.

10. Ibid.

11. Ibid.

12. Ibid.

13. Ibid.

Chapter 6. Going to the Florida Supreme Court

1. Jeffrey Toobin. *Too Close to Call: The Thirty-Six-Day Battle to Decide the 2000 Election*. New York: Random, 2001. Print. 123.

2. "Counting the Vote; Gore Spurns Victory by Votes 'in Error.'" *New York Times*. New York Times, 14 Nov. 2000. Web. 8 May 2012.

3. "Al Gore Calls for Meeting with Governor Bush, Hands Counts of Florida Ballots." *CNN.com*. CNN, 15 Nov. 2000. Web. 23 Mar. 2012.

4. Jeffrey Toobin. *Too Close to Call: The Thirty-Six-Day Battle to Decide the 2000 Election*. New York: Random, 2001. Print. 131.

5. Ibid.

6. Richard A. Oppel Jr. "Counting the Vote: The Supreme Court Justices; in Florida's State Government, Court Is a Democratic Enclave." *New York Times*. New York Times, 17 Nov. 2000. Web. 8 May 2012.

7. Jeffrey Toobin. *Too Close to Call: The Thirty-Six-Day Battle to Decide the 2000 Election*. New York: Random, 2001. Print. 136–137.

8. Mark Whitman, ed. *Florida 2000: A Sourcebook on the Contested Presidential Election*. Boulder: Lynne Rienner, 2003. 54. *Google Book Search*. Web. 10 May 2012.

Chapter 7. *Bush v. Palm Beach Canvassing Board*

1. "Presidential Election Laws." *US Electoral College*. Office of the Federal Register, n.d. Web. 8 May 2012.

2. "The United States Constitution." *House.gov*. Law Revision Counsel of the US House of Representatives, 20 Sept. 2004. Web. 9 May 2012.

3. "Presidential Election Laws." *US Electoral College*. Office of the Federal Register, n.d. Web. 8 May 2012.

4. "Bush Certified as Winner in Florida, but Final Outcome in Doubt." *New York Times*. New York Times, 26 Nov. 2000. Web. 9 May 2012.

5. Jake Tapper. *Down and Dirty: The Plot to Steal the Presidency*. New York: Hachette, 2001. N. pag. *Google Book Search*. Web. 10 May 2012.

6. Jeffrey Toobin. *The Nine: Inside the Secret World of the Supreme Court*. New York: Doubleday, 2007. Print. 153.

7. Linda Greenhouse. "Contesting the Vote: The Supreme Court; U.S. Supreme Court Presses 2 Sides on Vote Case." *New York Times*. New York Times, 2 Dec. 2000. Web. 9 May 2012.

8. "Supreme Court Transcripts." *ABC News*. ABC News Internet Ventures, Yahoo! - ABC News Network, 1 Dec. 2000. Web. 9 May 2012.

9. Ibid.

10. Brian Lamb, Susan Swain, and Mark Farkas, eds. *The Supreme Court: A C-SPAN Book Featuring the Justices in their Own Words*. New York: PublicAffairs, 2010. Print. 47.

11. E. J. Dionne Jr. and William Kristol, eds. Bush v. Gore: *The Court Cases and the Commentary*. Washington, DC: Brookings, 2001. Print. 52.

Chapter 8. The Contest

1. Julian M. Pleasants. *Hanging Chads: The Inside Story of the 2000 Presidential Recount in Florida*. New York: Palgrave Macmillan, 2004. Print. 4.

2. Martin Merzer and the staff of *The Miami Herald*. *The Miami Herald Report: Democracy Held Hostage*. New York: St. Martin's, 2001. Print. 161.

3. Scott Martelle. "Recusal in Seminole Supported." *Los Angeles Times*. Los Angeles Times, 11 Nov. 2000. Web. 9 May 2012.

4. "Counting the Vote; Excerpts from Interview with Vice President: 'Integrity of Democracy' at Stake." *New York Times*. New York Times, 27 Nov. 2000. Web. 9 May 2012.

5. Martin Merzer and the staff of *The Miami Herald*. *The Miami Herald Report: Democracy Held Hostage*. New York: St. Martin's, 2001. Print. 162.

6. Ibid. 163.

7. Jeffrey Toobin. *Too Close to Call: The Thirty-Six-Day Battle to Decide the 2000 Election.* New York: Random, 2001. Print. 196.

8. Julian M. Pleasants. *Hanging Chads: The Inside Story of the 2000 Presidential Recount in Florida.* New York: Palgrave Macmillan, 2004. Print. 53.

9. "Florida Election Trial Recesses after Nine Often-Esoteric Hours." *CNN.com.* CNN, 2 Dec. 2000. Web. 9 May 2000.

10. David Firestone. "Contesting the Vote: The Overview; Gore Asks Judge for New Tally but Bush Calls It Unjustified." *New York Times.* New York Times, 3 Dec. 2000. Web. 9 May 2012.

11. David Barstow and Somini Sengupta. "Contesting the Vote: The Scene; Hesitations, Introductions and Objections All Contribute to Sluggish Pace." *New York Times.* New York Times, 3 Dec. 2000. Web. 9 May 2012.

12. E. J. Dionne Jr. and William Kristol, eds. Bush v. Gore*: The Court Cases and the Commentary.* Washington DC: Brookings, 2001. Print. 55.

13. Ibid.

14. Ibid.

15. Jeffrey Toobin. *The Nine: Inside the Secret World of the Supreme Court.* New York: Doubleday, 2007. Print. 158.

16. Ibid. 186.

17. "Contesting the Vote; Supreme Court's Decision to Halt the Florida Recount." *New York Times.* New York Times, 10 Dec. 2000. Web. 23 Mar. 2012.

18. Ibid.

Chapter 9. *Bush v. Gore*

1. Linda Greenhouse. "Contesting the Vote: The Overview; *Bush v. Gore* Is Now in Hands of Supreme Court." *New York Times.* New York Times, 11 Dec. 2000. Web. 9 May 2012.

2. "Equal Justice Under Law." *LibertyTeamUSA.com.* Liberty Team USA, 2012. Web. 9 May 2012.

3. Clare Cushman. *Courtwatchers: Eyewitness Accounts in the Supreme Court History.* Lanham, MD: Rowman & Littlefield, 2011. Print. 147.

4. Brian Lamb, Susan Swain, and Mark Farkas, eds. *The Supreme Court: A C-SPAN Book Featuring the Justices in Their Own Words.* New York: PublicAffairs, 2010. Print. 188.

5. Linda Greenhouse. "Contesting the Vote: The Overview; *Bush v. Gore* Is Now in Hands of Supreme Court." *New York Times*. New York Times, 11 Dec. 2000. Web. 9 May 2012.

6. "Supreme Court Transcripts." *ABC News*. ABC News Internet Ventures, Yahoo! - ABC News Network, 11 Dec. 2000. Web. 9 May 2012.

7. Jeffrey Toobin. *Too Close to Call: The Thirty-Six-Day Battle to Decide the 2000 Election.* New York: Random House, 2001. Print. 259.

8. "*Bush v. Gore*, Official Transcript." *SFGate.com*. SF Gate, 12 Dec. 2000. Web. 9 May 2012.

9. Ibid.

10. Ibid.

11. Ibid.

12. Ibid.

13. Ibid.

14. Ibid.

15. Ibid.

16. Ibid.

17. E. J. Dionne Jr. and William Kristol, eds. Bush v. Gore: *The Court Cases and the Commentary.* Washington DC: Brookings, 2001. Print. 103–104.

18. Bush v. Gore. 531 US 98. *Supreme Court Collection*. Legal Information Inst., Cornell U Law School, n.d. Web. 9 May 2012.

19. Ibid.

20. Ibid.

21. Ibid.

22. Ibid.

23. Ibid.

24. Ibid.

25. E. J. Dionne Jr. and William Kristol, eds. Bush v. Gore: *The Court Cases and the Commentary.* Washington DC: Brookings, 2001. Print. 125.

26. Bush v. Gore. 531 US 98. *Supreme Court Collection*. Legal Information Inst., Cornell U Law School, n.d. Web. 9 May 2012.

27. Ibid.

28. Ibid.

29. Ibid.

30. Ibid.

Chapter 10. Justice Served or Election Stolen?

1. Jeffrey Toobin. *Too Close to Call: The Thirty-Six-Day Battle to Decide the 2000 Election.* Random: New York, 2001. Print. 269.

2. Richard L. Berke and Katharine Q. Seelye. "The 43rd President: The Vice President; Bush Pledges to be President for 'One Nation,' Not One Party; Gore, Conceding, Urges Unity." *New York Times*. New York Times, 14 Dec. 2000. Web. 9 May 2012.

3. "Florida Recount: Official Statements." *Issues2000.org*. Issues2000, n.d. Web. 9 May 2012.

4. Richard L. Berke and Katharine Q. Seelye. "The 43rd President: The Vice President; Bush Pledges to Be President for 'One Nation,' Not One Party; Gore, Conceding, Urges Unity." *New York Times*. New York Times, 14 Dec. 2000. Web. 9 May 2012.

5. David E. Sanger. "The 43rd President: The Texas Governor; Bush Pledges to Be President for 'One Nation,' Not One Party; Gore, Conceding, Urges Unity." *New York Times*. New York Times, 14 Dec. 2000. Web. 9 May 2012.

6. Ibid.

7. Vincent Bugliosi. *The Betrayal of America: How the Supreme Court Undermined the Constitution and Chose Our President.* New York: Thunder's Mouth/Nation, 2001. Print. 43.

8. Ibid.

9. Larry D. Kramer. "No Surprise, It's an Activist Court." *New York Times*. New York Times, 12 Dec. 2000. Web. 9 May 2012.

10. Ibid.

11. Ibid.

12. Nelson Lund. "The Unbearable Rightness of *Bush v. Gore*." Eds. Arthur J. Jacobson and Michel Rosenfeld. *The Longest Night: Polemics and Perspectives on Election 2000*. Berkeley: U of California P, 2002. 178. *Google Book Search*. Web. 10 May 2012.

13. Ibid.

14. Ibid.

15. Brian Lamb, Susan Swain, and Mark Farkas, eds. *The Supreme Court: A C-SPAN Book Featuring the Justices in Their Own Words*. New York: PublicAffairs, 2010. Print. 117.

16. E. J. Dionne Jr. and William Kristol, eds. Bush v. Gore: *The Court Cases and the Commentary*. Washington DC: Brookings, 2001. Print. 281.

17. "The Speech: Inauguration 2001." *PBS.org*. MacNeil/Lehrer Productions, 2012. Web. 10 May 2012.

18. Julian M. Pleasants. *Hanging Chads: The Inside Story of the 2000 Presidential Recount in Florida*. New York: Palgrave Macmillan, 2004. Print. 89.

19. Ibid. 90.

Chapter 11. The Legacy of *Bush v. Gore*

1. Brian Costello. "New Study Finds Election Law Litigation Remains at More than Double Rate Before 2000 Election; More Cases Shift from State Court to Federal Court." *LLS.edu*. Loyola Law School, 19 Feb. 2009. Web. 9 May 2012.

2. Felicity Barringer. "2 Media Groups Move to Examine Florida Votes." *New York Times*. New York Times, 10 Jan. 2001. Web. 9 May 2012.

3. Richard L. Hasen. "The Real Legacy of *Bush v. Gore*." *Slate*. Slate Group, 3 Dec. 2010. Web. 9 May 2012.

4. Adam Cohen. "Has *Bush v. Gore* Become the Case that Must Not Be Named?" *New York Times*. New York Times, 15 Aug. 2006. Web. 9 May 2012.

5. Bush v. Gore. 531 US 98. *Supreme Court Collection*. Legal Information Inst., Cornell U Law School, n.d. Web. 9 May 2012.

6. Jeffrey Toobin. "Precedent and Prologue." *The New Yorker*. Condé Nast, 6 Dec. 2012. Web. 9 May 2012.

7. Ibid.

8. Richard L. Hasen. "The Real Legacy of *Bush v. Gore*." *Slate*. Slate Group, 3 Dec. 2010. Web. 9 May 2012.

9. "2004 Presidential General Election Results - Florida." *USElectionAtlas.org*. David Leip, 2012. Web. 9 May 2012.

10. Richard L. Hasen. "The Real Legacy of *Bush v. Gore*." *Slate*. Slate Group, 3 Dec. 2010. Web. 9 May 2012.

INDEX

INDEX CONTINUED

About the Author

Christine Heppermann is a columnist and reviewer for *The Horn Book Magazine*. She contributed chapters to *A Family of Readers: The Book Lover's Guide to Children's and Young Adult Literature* and *Children's Books and Their Creators*. Her nonfiction picture book, *City Chickens,* was published in 2012. She has also published poetry in literary journals for adults. She has an MA in Children's Literature from Simmons College and an MFA in Writing for Children and Young Adults from Hamline University.

About the Consultant

Richard D. Friedman earned a BA and JD from Harvard University and a DPhil from Oxford University. He is the Alene and Allan F. Smith Professor of Law at University of Michigan Law School and an expert on Supreme Court history.